FRAMING THE ARTIST

A Social Portrait of Mid-American Artists

Jeffrey W. Riemer and Nancy A. Brooks
Department of Sociology
Wichita State University

UNIVERSITY
PRESS OF
AMERICA

To Carla and John.

CONTENTS

PREFACE

In the following chapters we provide a social portrait of Kansas artists - not only creators of "fine art" but design artists, art educators and art hobbyists. We compare and contrast these artists to portray how they became artists, how they create their art products, what their work means to them and the unique problems they face.

The information we present is drawn from extensive research using questionnaires on a sample of 173 artists, in-depth interviews with seven specially selected artists, and an exhaustive search of the existing literature on artists. Much of the information provided is in the artist's own words. From this, we feel, we present an accurate protrayal of the contemporary Mid-American artist in society.

This book is unique in two respects. First, it focuses on the artist as a worker. An occupational sociological perspective is applied to how artists make their occupational choice, how they are trained, the risks, problems and rewards in choosing an art career, and the socially based values of artists. We discuss how creating art involves a work process that is largely social in nature, and how the problems confronting artists as members of distinct occupational groups are socially based problems. Second, we employ a comparative approach that allows us to make clear distinctions between the similarities and differences of the four types of artists.

We believe that art students and artists must make choices as to how they can best ply their artistic skills. Our book discusses pathways (career lines) and the associated risks and problems as well as the rewards of these. We believe the sociological insights provided here will benefit artists and future artists.

We wish to thank Dr. John Simoni, Mary Sue Foster, Cynthia Moore Jones, and Barbara Hoffmann for their consultation on the research process. Roger Lyon and Lynn West assisted with the data analysis, and Margie Sheridan, Rita Benskin and Rita Harper prepared the preliminary manuscript. We also acknowledge the support of Wichita State University faculty and staff which facilitated our research and writing. Our special gratitude goes to Ruby Baresch for typing the final manuscript.

A PRELIMINARY SKETCH - AN INTRODUCTION

All artists are primarily workers. The myth of the artist as a struggling, romantic figure who creates masterpieces in impoverished seclusion, of course does not stand. As workers, artists expend considerable time and hard work to create their artistic products. Like most other occupations their work is not glamorous, mystical or romantic.

The nature of art work is like other varieties of work. Artistic occupations have a clear historical background that can be traced to its present status. A complex work organization exists where all art work is done. There is a work routine that artists follow that involves specific tasks and organization of effort. Artists, like other workers, have peak demand periods, times of inactivity, standard operating procedures, as well as "dry periods" or other fluctuations in their productive activity.

Being an artist requires occupational training, the learning of certain skills and knowledge in order to do the work. There are job demands, often influenced by changing techniques, materials and general technological innovation.

The work of an artist is praised or rejected according to the constantly changing public mood and with this appraisal the artist's status and morale are affected. A clear occupational status system exists and within it different artistic roles can emerge. Some artists have seniority within this status system while others are still working for recognition.

Novice artists are recruited into this occupational system and receive training from established regulars. They are evaluated as they learn and may be promoted to a higher status or demoted according to their performance.

Becoming an artist involves more than the learning of skills and techniques. Occupations have a culture, a special language, and a set of behaviors and values appropriate to the work. Artists also learn and internalize these, as part of their training. It is from this internalization that an occupational commitment arises.

Artists follow career lines as do other workers. Aspiring artists pass through distinct stages of advancement. Artistic status is designated through this vertical (or horizontal) mobility.

On another level, many artists belong to occupational associations that provide support, codes of ethics, and a collective understanding of the meaning of artistic work. These are not unlike other workers' unions, trade associations or professional associations.

We believe much can be learned by viewing the artist as a worker and the following chapters will reflect this orientation.

METHODS

The data reported here are based upon a sample of 173 mid-American artists - 38 (22%) fine artists, 49 (28%) design artists, 57 (33%) art educators, and 29 (17%) amateur artists. Fine artists are independents who earn the majority of their livelihood through their art work. Design artists work for art production corporations while art educators teach (and produce) art in established educational institutions. Amateur artists do art work as a hobby. The majority of our artists create their art through painting or drawing (50%) or graphics (23%). Others in our sample indicated they primarily create pottery (12%), sculpture (10%), jewelry (3%), or weaving (2%).

Our sample of artists is distributed evenly by sex and their ages range from 19 to 76 years of age. Most are married (72%), protestant (59%), white (97%), and well educated (85% have done some college work with 41% holding at least a Master's Degree).

An open-ended mailed questionnaire coupled with a selective number of in-depth interviews provide the data for this study. Artists were selected from various art association membership lists, faculty lists from college and university catalogues, employee lists from selected commercial establishments (such as Hallmark) and from personal contacts. We have no reason

2

to believe that our sample of artists differs significantly from those in other areas of the country.

Throughout these chapters we attempt to let our artists speak for themselves. Throughout the text direct quotations will be followed by numbers in parenthesis referring to a code number used in the analysis of anonymous survey data. Our primary research instrument, an open-ended questionnaire, allowed artists to respond to our questions in writing rather than through fixed choice responses. We use many of these verbatim comments to summarize our findings.

In addition, we conducted seven in-depth interviews with a variety of selected artists. Each interview was tape recorded and lasted about two hours. We use the verbatim comments of these artists in a similar manner and devote one chapter (V) to their comments on a variety of selected issues that we feel will benefit other artists and future artists as well as the academic community.

OVERVIEW

Chapter II, PREPARING THE PALETTE - BECOMING AN ARTIST, focuses on the recruitment, training and resultant commitment artists have to their work. A comparative analysis of occupational socialization is provided by type of artist.

Chapter III, PAINTING THE PORTRAIT - DOING ART WORK, provides a work process model that was developed from the data to illustrate how artists progress from an initial idea to the completion and evaluation of their art products. A comparative analysis of this work process is provided for different types of artists.

Chapter IV, YES, BUT IS IT "ART"? - ARTIST's VALUES,[1] employs the concepts autonomy, inner-directedness and other-directedness to compare the value orientations by type of artist. A comparative analysis is used to show how artists' values influence their art work and their attitudes toward art.

Chapter V, IN THEIR OWN WORDS, consists of selected verbatim comments by seven artists in various artistic careers. Here the emphasis is on comments that will benefit artists and future artists. Topics addressed include: establishing a reputation, defining good art, advice to art students, comments on "dry" and "dark" periods, among others. Commenting are Black Bear Bosin, Dee Connett, Robert Kiskadden, Paula Krekovich, Charles Sanderson, Nick Vaccaro, and Fran Wagner.

Chapter VI, FINDING SPACE IN THE GALLERY - EPILOGUE, focuses on the role of the artist in contemporary society. Historical insight is employed to illuminate the causes of the increased alienation many artists have experienced. An alternative role model is suggested that would enable contemporary artists to maintain their integrity while pursuing fulfillment in their artistic work.

An ANNOTATED BIBLIOGRAPHY is included at the end of this book with detailed summaries of 31 articles and books pertaining to art as an occupational pursuit.

NOTE
[1]A modified version of this chapter appeared in 1979 (see Brooks and Riemer, 1979).

II.

PREPARING THE PALETTE - BECOMING AN ARTIST

Art as an occupation has always been a chancy venture. Few make it as established artists and for those
who do their reputations are often short lived (Griff,
1960, 1964; Levine, 1972). Unlike most occupational
selections the choice to become an artist is a risky
one (Fox, 1957).

Career lines are easily blocked, highly competitive, and often based upon contemporary vogue. Few
artists survive as independent, self sufficient pro-
ducers of art work (Christopherson, 1974; Becker,
1974). Most are forced downward in the occupational
structure of the art industry, forced to work within an
institutional framework. Others are economically rele-
gated to the level of hobbyist ("Sunday painter")
(Goodman, 1974). Reputations are difficult to estab-
lish and even more difficult to maintain (Griff, 1964a,
1968; Burnham, 1973).

To become an artist, to conceive of one's self as
an artist, appears to be a tension ridden process.
Learning to do art work requires arduous training while
a clear and firm occupational commitment may be difficult to achieve (Griff, 1964; Strauss, 1970). But how
does the process of becoming an artist and the resultant occupational commitment to one's work vary across
occupational lines?

We explore this process by focusing on four types
of artists: fine artists, art educators, design (commercial) artists, and amateur artists (those who dabble
in art work as a hobby). We search out the differences
and similarities between these types of artists to illuminate how occupational identification develops and
how career contingencies influence this process.

RECRUITMENT

Occupational choice stems from a complex and inter-
related set of elements. Alternatives based upon opportunity, knowledge, and ability are gradually nar-
rowed. Recruits are funneled into certain occupations
over others by the social circumstances they encounter.
Social characteristics, family background influences,
and educational experiences (and some would add "pure

chance") provide the basis for occupational recrutiment (Braude, 1975).

Careers in art begin here. Teachers, parents, and friends provide the necessary encouragement, and the "track through time" toward an artistic occupation begins. We explore this process by focusing on the decision to become an artist and the influences that brought about that decision.

DECISION

When did our artists decide to become artists?

For some, the choice to become an artist was no choice at all. They simply felt it was innate. As one artist put it,

> I am not sure that anyone decides to become an artist. I always knew that I had a better than average ability to put down an idea on paper with a drawing or painting instrument. I got a lot of satisfaction from this and it developed and evolved. (070)

Seventeen percent of our artists responded this way with each type about equally represented.

Others made their choice prior to their educational training (7%) or long after they had their educational training (16%). The majority, however, made their decision prior to high school (31%) or during high school or college (29%).

When we compare type of artist with their decision to embark on this career line we find that design artists typically make their decision by the time they graduate from high school (57%). The other types of artists are less clear in their decision. Most fine artists made their choice in either elementary school (24%), during college (21%), or long after their educational training (28%). In general, design artists and art educators made their decisions for a career in art slightly earlier than fine artists and amateur artists decided later than the rest.

This can be explained, in part, by the relatively stable career lines for both design artists and art educators. Both must sacrifice some of their artistic freedom for the security provided by an institutional

6

framework. Design artists may begin working in a studio prior to graduation from high school, and their formal educational training in the skills and techniques of their trade is frequently coupled with "on the job" training (Griff, 1960).

Similarly, art educators know exactly what is expected of them in order to begin teaching art. They must master various art skills and techniques through course work at a college or university and as students they typically begin practice teaching (Strauss, 1970). A Master of Fine Arts degree is well recognized as their terminal degree. If clear guidelines exist, if persons realize exactly what they need to do to become a certain type of worker, we may expect their choices (or decisions) to occur somewhat earlier.

The career lines for fine artists are much less certain. Griff (1960:219) has estimated "the number of those who are able to support themselves exclusively from the sale of their paintings in this country ranges from five to fifteen persons." Thus, art work may have to remain a hobby. As one amateur artist put it:

> I only work in between family and civic demands on my time. I take advantage of any opportunity to learn and produce art work as time allows. (I began only) after my children were old enough to give me enough free time to pursue my studies. (096)

This artist reflects the difficulty in sustaining an avid interest in art activities when faced with conflicting obligations.

Fine artists typically face increasing uncertainty and no job prospects after extensive educational training (not to mention the time and money involved). They may be forced to work at an undesirable job to support themselves and allow for the pursuit of their independent art work. Others may marry and let their spouse support their art activities (Rosenberg and Fliegel, 1965). Thus, the choices to embark on this career line may require considerably more contemplation.

INFLUENCES

What influences artists to become artists?

Our artists indicated that the primary influences in their choice to become artists were their own talent and interest (28%) and their teachers' encouragment (23%). The responses were similar for all types of artists with art educators placing slightly more emphasis on both. One art educator described the influences affecting his choice as, "A good art teacher and a vital interest in the subject for a long time." (039)

And similarly, a design artist indicated:

> My teachers in grade school and junior high and also my relatives encouraged my decision to be a professional artist by realizing I had talent and complimenting me for my talents. But I don't feel that I would have actually become a professional artist if I didn't enjoy it as much as I do and feeling that it is the thing that I do best. (159)

Parents and other relatives provided only a slight influence, especially for fine artists. Other artists and friends provided the least influence. These are, however, explicitly stated influences. If we look at certain implicit social influences, we find that specific relationships emerge.

Sex

Although our sample is evenly distributed by sex, more females were found among the fine artists (63%) and amateur artists (57%). Design artists were equally distributed by sex but more males were found among the art educators (66%). We feel this variation may reflect a sexual bias for certain art careers that stems from the risk involved with these choices. Females may, given the possible alternative of marriage, be more inclined to choose a more risky career in fine art. On the other hand, males may be more inclined to choose a safer career in art education. Educational institutions may also be more inclined to hire males.

Age

The mean (average) age for all of our artists is 42 years of age. This closely paralleled the mean age of the amateur artists ($\overline{X} = 44$) and the fine artists, who were slightly older ($\overline{X} = 46$). Design artists were the youngest category ($\overline{X} = 34$) and the art educators the

TABLE 1

DEMOGRAPHIC CHARACTERISTICS OF ARTISTS

		Fine Artist	Design Artist	Art Educator	Amateur Artist	Total
		(N=38)	(N=49)	(N=67)	(N=29)	(N=173)
Sex		F 63%	M F 50%	M 66%	F 57%	M F 50%
Age		X̄ 46	X̄ 34	X̄ 58	X̄ 44	X̄ 42
Marital Status*	Single	5%	20%	20%	19%	17%
	Married	74	74	70	70	72
	Divorced/Separated	13	6	9	7	9
Religion	Protestant	61	63	51	66	60
	Catholic	8	10	20	4	12
	Other	10	9	13	12	11
	None	21	18	16	18	17

*Widowed Category not shown.

9

oldest ($\overline{X} = 58$). In part, we feel this variation reflects the different educational requirements for the artists. It is possible to become a design artist at a relatively young age, whereas an art educator may require six years of college. For some artists, art education may represent a position that they drift into as they become older and more concerned with occupational security. In the same respect, design art may represent an occupation that some artists drift out of as they become older and seek more purely creative work.

Marital Status

Although the majority of our artists are married, fine artists differ from the others with the lowest percentage of single persons (5%) and the highest percentage of those divorced or separated (13%). We feel some of this variation may reflect the added stress and tension associated with being a fine artist. Some fine artists may be more inclined toward divorce or separation because of the unconventional life style they may follow. Other fine artists may be more inclined to marry and receive some financial support from the work of their spouse (Rosenberg and Fliegal, 1965).

Religion

Although the majority of our artists are protestant, a relatively high percentage (18%) indicated they were atheists or agnostics. This was generally consistent for each type of artist but highest for fine artists. Again, we feel this may reflect the unconventional life style sometimes found among artists since artistic values may conflict with traditional values.

Social Class

The social class milieu in which a person is reared represents a major social influence upon occupational aspirations. We measure social class by parental education and parental occupation. Griff (1968) suggests that parents enthusiastically introduce and promote art interests in their children, stressing humanistic and hobbyist values. This enthusiasm stops, however, if their child displays an interest in pursuing an art career. This is true for all class strata but is most applicable for the middle class, from which most artists

10

TABLE 2

SOCIAL CLASS CHARACTERISTICS OF ARTISTS

	Fine Artist % (N=38)	Design Artist % (N=49)	Art Educator % (N=57)	Amateur Artist % (N=29)	Total % (N=173)
Father's Education Level					
Less than High School	32	15	33	22	26
High School	41	48	46	44	45
College	27	37	22	34	29
Father's Occupation					
White Collar	50	53	48	35	48
Blue Collar	50	47	52	65	52
Mother's Education Level					
Less than High School	19	11	29	18	20
High School	59	72	60	52	62
College	22	17	11	30	18
Mother's Occupation					
White Collar	28	29	22	33	28
Blue Collar	10	26	17	15	17
Housewife	62	45	61	52	55

arise.   According to Griff (1968:147),

> An artistic career is not generally initiated
> by an education at a prep school or an elite
> college, nor do persons of low economic stand-
> ing usually become artists by emulating models
> found in their communities (they are far more
> likely to emulate athletes).

Our artists tend to emerge from a middle class
background.   Their fathers and mothers typically have
a high school education.   If either of the parents do
have a college education it is more likely to be the
father.   Similarly, the occupations of artists' fathers
tend to cluster in the middle range, while the majority
of their mothers are housewives (Rosenberg and Fliegal,
1965).   We do find, however, that 6% of the fathers and
6% of the mothers have art or art related occupations
such as architect, fashion designer, musician, or photographer.

When we compare type of artist to father's occupation we find that more art educators have fathers in
the professions (32%) while design artists' fathers
work in managerial positions (31%).   The fathers of our
amateur artists tend to be craftsmen or foremen (26%)
whereas the fathers of fine artists display no clear
clustering.

Collectively, this set of implicit social influences provides a social basis for better understanding
why these artists chose their particular art career.
But before we can begin to fully integrate these influences we must focus on the actual training of our artists.

TRAINING

Occupational socialization is the process by which
an initiate is transformed into a regular (Moore, 1969;
Hughes, 1971; Riemer, 1977).   Necessary skills and techniques are gradually learned and at least minimally in-
ternalized.   Training occurs in formal educational sit-
uations and through actual performance.   The hopeful
trainee is processed: shaped in the ways and means of
working.   Proficiency is learned through practice and
time.

The public school system is the chief mechanism

for pumping a flow of talent into art today (Griff, 1968). Teachers (elementary and high school) direct promising students to possible careers in art. Art schools or colleges and universities that offer specialties in art receive these interested students. Strauss (1970:159-160) has suggested that:

> ...art schools, unlike engineering and medical schools, do not prepare students for a single occupation but for a very loosely related family of occupations and specialties....Art schools function to instill standards and artistic values to teach techniques and skills.

Since few students at entrance know much about art, these schools are geared to diversification. Art educators, fine artists, design artists, and others (collectors, hobbyists and educated consumers) emerge from this broad based context. For first year students, the courses are usually the same. It is only in the later years that specialties, and consequently identities, begin to emerge.

Difficulties also emerge. Role conflicts exist between different art careers. For some students (and teacher-artists) fine art is the only true art form. Design art is no art at all and art education is merely a compromise position. An implicit rule in art school for those majoring in art education is "to not let anyone know about it." Design artists are typically outcasts (Griff, 1960, 1964, 1968; Strauss, 1970).

Part of this variation between different artistic pursuits is reflected in the amount of formal education required for each and the rigidity of course content. Our artists reflect these differences.

Educational Level

The majority of our artists are very well educated with 78% holding at least one college degree. As we would expect the art educators have the most formal education with the majority holding a graduate degree (86%). They are followed by the design artists with the majority holding a college degree (74%). The amateur artists follow with the fine artists having the least formal higher education (59%).

13

TABLE 3

EDUCATIONAL LEVEL AND MAJOR OF ARTISTS

	Fine Artist %(N=38)	Design Artist %(N=49)	Art Educator %(N=57)	Amateur Artist %(N=29)	Total %(N=173)
Educational Level Completed:					
High School	38	26	3	33	22
College	35	66	11	45	37
Graduate Degree	24	8	86	22	41
Educational Major:					
Art related	69	97	98	69	87
Non-Art Related	31	3	2	31	13

14

Educational Major

The majority of all types of artist were art or art related (art history, music, architecture) majors. More art educators (98%) and design artists (97%) were art or art related majors than were fine artists (69%) or amateur artists (69%).

Art school serves as a sorting device for placing artists into a variety of vocations or avocations. Some of these require a rather long, structured period of formal training as with art educators, while others are less time consuming but similarly structured, as with design artists. Others are much more flexible in terms of time required and rigidity of curriculum. The education of fine artists and amateur artists tends to be of this latter variety. But becoming an artist of any type requires some commitment on the part of the student. All art education is highly specialized. However, educational training alone is not enough; to be an artist is to identify oneself as an artist and to be involved in activities surrounding one's work.

COMMITMENT

Occupational commitment develops gradually through time. A person begins to identify with a particular line of work while investing of himself or herself in that work. As basic skills are mastered and established workers begin to accept, as members, new artists who are identifying themselves as art workers. Occupational commitment is established through occupational identification (Becker, 1960; Becker and Carper, 1956; Becker and Strauss, 1956).

Becoming a member of an occupation can mean the occupation becomes an intricate and inseparable part of one's life. We feel this is true for most artists.

Our artists not only do art, they "live" art. On a social level, they frequently discuss art with other artists (95%), friends (80%), and relatives (63%). On a personal level, they own the art work of other artists (95%), keep abreast of the work of other artists (91%), frequently read art magazines (86%), and frequently attend art shows where their own work is not on display (90%).

This occupational commitment is similar for each

TABLE 4

OCCUPATIONAL COMMITMENT OF ARTISTS

	Fine Artist	Design Artist	Art Educator	Amateur Artist	Total
	%	%	%	%	%
	(N=38)	(N=49)	(N=57)	(N=29)	(N=173)
Frequently discuss art with:					
Artists	92	98	95	97	95
Friends	89	72	81	86	80
Relatives	67	54	62	77	63
Own work of other artists	98	90	97	96	95
Keep up with the work of other artists	95	89	96	82	91
Frequently read art magazines	90	70	97	89	86
Frequently attend art shows where their own art is not on display	87	86	95	89	90

16

type of artist. Design artists frequently discuss art with other artists but less with friends and relatives. Perhaps this is because they work in close proximity with other artists. Amateur artists are more inclined to discuss art with other artists as well as friends and relatives. On a social level amateur artists are more committed to their art work and design artists are less committed than the others but these variations are slight.

On a more personal level the art educators display the highest commitment. They are more likely to keep up with the work of other artists, frequently read art magazines, and attend art shows where their own work is not on display. A high percentage of them own the work of other artists (97%). The design artists are the least committed on this personal level. They identify somewhat less with their occupation than do the others, but again these variations are slight.

DISCUSSION

We have traced a number of important similarities and differences among a sample of different types of artists. These reflect how occupational identification emerges and how it is influenced by career contingencies facing these artists. Each type of artist is drawn from a different social context, faces a different training process, and ends up identifying somewhat differently with their chosen occupation.

Most artists share many social characteristics with other occupational groups. They were reared in middle class families, are married, express religious affiliation, are well educated, and undergo rigorous occupational training. They are also likely to specialize within their occupation and to experience different problems appropriate to each specialty. Fine artists face financial insecurity and high competition. Art educators face problems associated with academe, and design artists face similar problems associated with "art production shops." Becoming an artist is not simply a matter of exercising one's talent.

Fine artists operate under considerably more stress and uncertainty than the others and follow a training sequence that is less structured, but in the end they appear to be more committed to their work and activities surrounding their work than some of the others.

Design artists have a much clearer career line to follow but end up displaying less commitment to their occupation. Art educators face a more rigid training sequence than others and emerge strongly committed to their work. Amateur artists are somewhat unique. They typically begin their careers much later, have a rather flexible training sequence but end up strongly committed to their work on a social level. Art as a hobby appears to provide a great deal of personal satisfaction without the tensions and compromises found in other artistic pursuits.

Different art careers present different problems for artists. Fine artists are faced with the most risk, tension and uncertainty, while amateur artists face the least. Art education and design art represent alternate compromise positions. Art educators are not only artists, they are faculty members, and consequently are faced with the constraints and expectations associated with that dual position (Gosnell, 1976; Risenhoover and Blackburn, 1976). Design artists face comparable problems by working in "production plants." Their creative work emerges from a nine to five schedule, five days per week (Griff, 1960). Both design artists and art educators have less time to pursue their own creative work.

Yet there is a leveling effect that emerges here. A very high degree of occupational commitment exists across occupational lines. If commitment to one's occupation is viewed as the degree of personal involvement in activities surrounding the occupation, artists display a shared interest in art that takes precedence over specific occupational differences. A common "central life interest" emerges for artists. Commitment to art creates a social bond between varieties of artists and may in fact represent what is called the "art world." Although different art careers are structured by different social matrixes and occupational (and avocational) distinctions do prevail, all artists appear to unify through their identification with their art work.

PAINTING THE PORTRAIT - DOING ART WORK

It is no secret that people spend the major share of their lives working. We know what work is, what most workers do, and what work means for a functioning society. We train for work from an early age, practice working for a large portion of our lives, and finish-up by reflecting on our work accomplishments. Working remains a universal activity, a necessary and highly respected activity in any society. But do we understand how people work?

Moore (1969) suggests that work may focus on producing products, generating ideas, or providing services. Certainly any work activity may be shown to be unlike another in terms of what is produced, developed, or provided. But is there a general work process common to all varieties of work activity? Do all workers regardless of what they work on, at, or with utilize a shared process to accomplish their unique products, ideas, or services? We believe they do.

Our argument centers on artists but is not limited to them. Artists have always been considered a unique type of worker. The work of artists has traditionally stood as a prototype of labor that is free and non-forced. Through an exercise of special insight and technical expertise artists display creativity. Their artistic constructions will provide a richness of detail for our systematic delineation of the work process.

THE PROCESS OF WORKING

Working is very much a social activity in that workers through their labor actually construct a social reality. Their outpourings provide the material backdrop for social life, the texture of social relationships, and the cultural knowledge necessary to perpetuate society.

We believe a general work process is a theme that cuts across all occupations. Working regardless of the accomplishments involved, requires a person to mentally and physically work through a series of stages toward that accomplishment. This is essentially a dialectical

19

process in which the worker "muddles through" a sequence of rational steps continually modifying his strategy along the way. A completed product, idea, or service emerges from this process. Workers generate these outcomes through sweat, excitement, stress, and in some unfortunate cases - boredom.

The model generated by Berger and Luckman (1967) provides a general framework for our discussion. Here working can be viewed as an unending dialectical process. Products, ideas, and services that emerge through the activity of work can be shown to develop through this process. Workers begin from an existing reality, reappropriate some of this "objective reality" and modify it into a newly created reality. This mixture of manual and mental ingredients is characteristic of any work activity.

Workers regardless of what they are working on, at, or with are outpouring themselves into the world (externalization). In turn, their products, ideas, or services take on a reality of their own (objectivation). And these same products, ideas, or services are selectively reappropriated into the mental constructions of others (internalization). Working becomes an activity that is continually in transformation, an unending process of expansion, refinement, and modification. New products are developed from the insights culled from the old. Better ideas emerge through the integration of other ideas. And improved services are enriched by tried practices.

By analyzing how artists work we are able to delineate this work process, following it step-by-step from the stimulus of an idea to the evaluation of a finished art product.

Figure 1 will serve as an orientation model for the ensuing discussion of how artists work.

Internalization

Internalization is the reappropriation of existing reality, transforming it from structures of the objective world into structures of the person's subjective consciousness (Berger, 1969:4). It is through this process of internalization that workers reappropriate selected aspects of their real world into structures of their mental creations. This is a transitional phase

20

FIGURE 1

THE WORK PROCESS

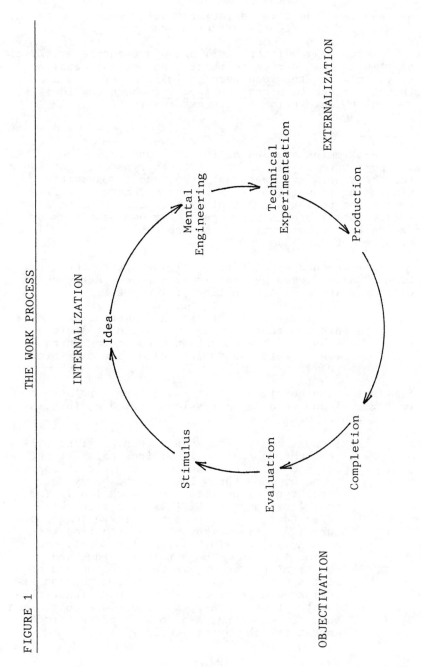

between the objective, existing reality and the creation of a new, slightly different reality.

Three stages in the work process occur here: first,
a stimulus that serves to inspire an idea, second, a
stage in which the idea becomes fully developed, and
third, a stage of mental engineering where the idea is
thought through prior to its externalization.

Stimulus

A stimulus arouses or inspires one to action. This
is the source of all ideas. Artists typically get ideas
for their work from personal experience, observation
(including travel), or from nature. Others keep files
containing photos and clippings that they turn to for
ideas. Still others rely upon their own past work or
the work of other artists. As one artist put it, "I
steal a lot!" (143)

A frequent response from all artists to the question, "Where do you get the ideas for your art work?"
was "Everywhere." As one fine artist put it:

> After years of painting and sketching my eyes
> are constantly in an idea-stimulus awareness.
> I have become conditioned to seeing things
> (those which stimulate me) as a media (sic).
> (017)

Similarly, another fine artist - a potter - relates how
past visual and reading impressions served as inspiration for his work:

> I envision my mind as a screen, a giant fil-
> ter, through which all visions pass. I sel-
> ect and store unconsciously those that appeal
> to me or lend themselves to the heavy, struc-
> tural type of 3-dimensional work I do. The
> most exciting type of idea...is that which I
> refer to as an "image pot." These images oc-
> cur at any time...but mostly at a time when
> my mind is relaxing....I will suddenly see
> flashed upon my mind screen a unique and
> beautiful pot form....Within the subsequent
> millisecond, I will also envision the compli-
> cations and intricacies of such an innovative
> construction process, and the glaze colors and
> body textures that are to be used to form and
> accent its character. (052)

This latter illustration carries us somewhat beyond the stimulus situation and captures the mental processing of an idea. The stimulus is the beginning stage of the work process; it "triggers" ideas. (083) It is a "flash" of intuitive thought. (059)

Design artists are faced with a slightly different situation. Unlike the other types of artists they are expected to satisfy the desires of their clients or employers. They often begin by talking with clients and determining their needs. As one design artist put it, "budget determines how much think time you have." (117)

Consequently, design artists typically rely upon files for their ideas. Photographs, magazine articles, post cards, newspaper clippings, television shows, museum displays, books, greeting cards, poems, and quotations are frequently mentioned idea sources. They literally store these for future use. Since their work often requires rapid transition from idea to finished product, and being continually faced with deadlines, production schedules and the like, they must often force this process instead of waiting for ideas to occur. As one design artist put it, "We're influenced by the job ticket." (163)

Art educators also display a difference in the source of their ideas. More than the other types of artists they rely on their past work for an inspiration for future work. They frequently mention working "on a series" (005) or that one idea develops or "grows from another." (010)

Amateur artists appear less concerned by when or how they become stimulated. "Certain things just strike a chord" (097) is a common response. Given that time pressures are removed from the work of amateur artists, they are able to let things happen. They are in a position to wait for "a visual stimulus or incident to trigger a creative impulse." (046)

Although artists start from different sources they are inspired in much the same way. They are aroused by what might prove to be the beginning of a good idea. And it is from these ideas that their creative images arise.

Most artists agree that it requires constant work to be inspired. It is not something you sit back and wait for. The well known contemporary artist, Jamie

23

Wyeth, commented on this when asked how many hours each day he spent painting:

> Almost all day. I mean this bit about having to be inspired is a pretty pile of crap. It's like anything else. You've got to keep at it. You keep your tools sharpened and wait for the day when all of a sudden things start clicking (People Weekly 1974:56).

Idea

An idea rises full blown from a stimulus. It is a mental construct; an image that conveys meaning and feeling. The idea represents a realization for the artist of what might turn out to be a future artistic product. This transition from stimulus to idea was described by one fine artist as "a feeling (inspiration) developed into an idea (visualized)." (017)

The idea stage in the work process is a clarifying step. Feelings are firmed-up into a mental image that has substance and body. You have "something to work with," is the way an art educator put it. (087)

All artists appreciate ideas and need them in order to work. Regardless of the type of artist this idea stage is a period of excitement. They frequently mention being so overwhelmed with an idea that it becomes difficult to do anything else. They work feverishly to capture it. A fine artist stated he has had ideas that were so exciting that he "couldn't wait to get it down on paper." (095)

Design artists are less dramatic about this. They emphasize the time pressures they work under and the clients they must please. According to one design artist:

> When I am given an assignment, or start an idea on my own, it mulls around in my head. The design kind of works itself around in the back of my head, while I spend my conscious time on setting parameters, gathering details on processes and limitations, and the medium to use. (170)

The idea is the real starting point for all art work. An art educator referred to it as an "incubation

24

period." (099)   It does not guarantee a finished product
nor does it provide the full details necessary for that
product to emerge.   It is a conception "in the mind's
eye" according to a design artist (091) and this conception evolves in modified form as the artist works.

Most artists agree that being too critical at the
moment an idea develops could inhibit full expression
of it.   Most feel judgment should be totally suspended
while the creative process flows.   A bad idea can always be thrown out.

Mental Engineering

The mental engineering stage requires the artist
to determine the details for subsequent work.   This is
the planning stage where the artist decides how the
idea can best be transformed into an artistic product.
Alternative approaches are considered with crucial decisions being made along the way.   Questions are asked
and answered, media are chosen, and finished products
are imagined - all before any physical work takes place.
Here the "idea, or thought, is painted in my mind," said
one fine artist. (129)

This is the thinking stage in the work process and
it is a critical stage.   Ideas die here if the artist
cannot envision how substance can be given to that idea.
As an art educator put it, "An idea is pushed to see
what happens to it." (113)   This is a mentally taxing
period composed of a great deal of "imagining" what
might be. (107)   Most artists agree that this is a time
consuming stage with the actual production of the product taking far less time or effort.   A fine artist reflected that he often "loses interest in a piece if
(he) think(s) about it too long" and the idea may be
stored for later use or dropped altogether. (083)

But this stage is at the heart of creative work.
The artist considers a range of possibilities for the
realization of his envisioned product.   All options can
be evaluated: the view, the size, the style, the media.
Each of these, according to a design artist, are viewed
in relationhip to the purpose of the piece and always
present is the question, "What do I want to show?" (111)
And this view is seconded by an art educator:

> There is an extensive search for precisely
> the right form - a paring away or rejection
> of all that is superfluous or untrue - an

> intellectual, emotional, and visual explora-
> tion of all the possibilities - a sort of
> open headed casting about for the visual ele-
> ments needed. (100)

Along these same lines Getzels and Csikszentmihalyi
(1977) have suggested that most creative artists remain
open in their thinking and operate without fixed assump-
tions. When art students were compared for their creativity it was the future fine artists that agonized
over their formulations for an artistic product while
future design artists passed through this formulation
stage quickly and completed the product. Their findings suggest that highly creative persons in any field
are "problem finders" not "problem solvers."

Each of these early stages are necessary for subsequent work to occur. The stimulus provides the inspiration that in turn can bloom into a solid idea and
the idea is mentally engineered to determine all details
for what is to transpire. Collectively these three
stages in the work process represent an internalization
of selective features from existing reality. Artists
reappropriate from their existing reality, transforming
objective features into new creations of their subjective consciousness. And within this sequence, as with
the stages to follow, a constant dialectical process is
taking place. We can now move to the next sequence of
stages in this work process.

Externalization

Externalization is the constant outpouring of both
mental and physical activities into the world (Berger,
1969:4). It is through the process of externalization
that workers express themselves through their products,
ideas, or services. This is a transitional phase between the reality that has been reappropriated and the
reality that will be newly created.

Two stages in the work process occur here: first,
a technical experimentation in which the previous mental constructions are implemented, and second, the production stage where the product, idea, or service is
actualized.

Technical Experimentation

After an artist has worked out the details of how

26

a piece is to be done, he or she must implement those thoughts. The technical experimentation stage is a time to see if what was thought would work actually does work. An art educator referred to this as a "trial composition" stage. (108)

Here the artist works to express an idea materially, roughly at first, then with added refinement. This is a tedious period where artists draw upon all their skill and expertise to create their envisioned product materially. According to one fine artist:

> (I) sketch my interpretation loosely, then make up my palette of colors, paint the canvas here and there, measuring values, colors against each other, and adjusting lines to make a pleasing composition. (004)

Similarly, a design artist reflects on her method:

> I will do sketches, thinking and working with the elements, piecing them into a composition. Then I choose the version that is most interesting, exciting and stimulating and I complete it. (172)

This stage in the work process is characterized by a continual shaping and reshaping "until it is right." (024) Some refer to it as a "trial and error" period (044) where errors and weaknesses are culled away and a new version is created. There is "constant shifting, sorting and decision making" (175), a continual "striving for perfection." (161) It is from this labor that the actual production of the art product emerges.

Production

The production stage flows naturally from the technical experimentation stage. It is not a difficult transition for the artist. In fact, some artists argue that "if the process is authentic the art creates itself." (092) This is the execution period and it occurs naturally. According to an art educator, it is a natural part of "building to a climax." (108)

The artist is relaxed during this period. Every detail has been carefully and thoroughly worked out and the artist is satisfied with the decisions that have been made. All that remains is the final execution of the product.

This is a pleasant time for the artist. After wavering periods of joy, tension, and hard work all that remains is "finishing up the details." (175) Yes, some are concerned if their "article will sell" (002) or if others will appreciate their work, but all express pleasure in the final actualization of their idea.

Unfortunately some design artists are removed from the actual production stage and a set of specialists take over. A design artist relates how his product is finished by others:

> After an O.K., it is graphically produced in the form of mechanical art. This in turn is shot by a camera, stripped by the negative department, plates made, run on a press, and finally the end product is finished, bound and ready for delivery. (014)

These middle stages in the work process are where the actual observable work activity takes place. The technical experimentation stage provides the first implementation of an idea into concrete form and the production stage provides the final thrust toward a completed product. Collectively these two stages in the work process represent an externalization of the worker's subjective consciousness into the real world. Here, artists spill out their internal creations back into reality. And as in the sequence before and the sequence to follow a constant dialectical process is occurring. There is an ever-present drive toward integration and synthesis. We now move to the final sequence in the work process.

Objectivation

Objectivation is the attainment by the products of this activity (both physical and mental) of a reality of their own (Berger, 1969:4). It is through the process of objectivation that the products, ideas, or services of workers emerge as distinct entities separate from their creators. They take on a reality "sui generis" (in and of themselves). This is a transitional phase between the creating of reality and the recreating (or modification) of that same reality.

Two stages in the work process occur here: first, completion of the product, thought or service, and second, evaluation of the result by the worker-creator

28

and others.

Completion

The finished product represents the end of the work process. It is the "climax" according to an art educator. (108) It occurs when "one gives birth to his work of art," said a fine artist. (042)

The completion stage is a state of accomplishment. Frustrations, tensions and stresses now subside as the artist is freed from his creation. It stands on its own apart from and external to its creator. A fine artist expresses her understanding of this final stage:

> Once a fabric or drawing is complete it's as though it has a life of its own. It exists apart from me. (173)

This is a joyous time for the artist, a culmination of creative effort and a sharing of this effort with the outside world. A fine artist captures this emotion laden stage:

> There is agony and doubt, and there is satisfaction and joy that you have done your best...and are pleased and proud of the result. (042)

The product of an arduous process now exists on its own. It is offered to the world and for better or worse becomes part of that world. Removed from the hands and influence of the artist-creator, the product exists as a distinct entity. It is no longer shielded from the view of others.

Evaluation

When the finished piece emerges it is evaluated by others. For the artist-creator these may include: clients, art consumers, students, other artists, art dealers, exhibit judges, or friends and relatives. Here the product is scrutinized and critically appraised. Evaluations are made as to its quality and worth.

The artist, of course, plays a part in this evaluation, perhaps even choosing who the first evaluators will be. And the artist is affected by these evaluations for they will reflect from his or her product and onto their conception of self. Favorable evaluations will enhance the worth of the product and the name of the artist. Unfavorable evaluations will detract from the same. But regardless of the outcome, the art product now exists as part of reality and it is from this reality that reappropriations are made.

This final sequence in the work process separates the worker from his or her created product. The completion stage finalizes the work effort and the evaluation stage appraises that effort. Collectively these two stages in the work process represent an objectivation by the product of the worker's activity. Here, artists send forth the fruits of their labor into the marketplace.

We have delineated the work process for artists. This began with a "flash" of intuitive thought (stimulus), generated into a firm image in the "mind's eye" (idea), and was shaped and refined in artistic detail (mental engineering). From this internalization phase the idea was tried and modified (technical experimentation) and finally constructed (production). This externalization phase brought forth a finished product (completion) that would face the scrutiny of others (evaluation). This end product exists apart from the artist who created it. It remains objectified and ready for reappropriation.

We have provided a detailed analysis of how artists work. This does not mean, of course, that all artistic work culminates in a finished product. Our artists tell us that many of their creative ventures are abandoned or destroyed along the way. As one fine artist informed us:

> I might destroy a work before it is ever completed if it is unsatisfactory. Therefore, it would never be finished, and would only be a study in mind for the future - and might never develop into a finished piece, or develop at a much later date. (080)

This shows us how ever-changing the work process is. Workers seem to "muddle through" this process, integrating and synthesizing their thoughts as they go, and if everything does gel a completed product (idea or service) may emerge.

DISCUSSION

At the heart of all work activity is a shared work process. Regardless of what is produced, what thoughts become crystalized, or what services are provided, all workers utilize the very same process in their work.

For some workers this process is completely within their control and they experience the entire sequence of stages. For others the full sequence is interrupted and they are forced to rely upon others to accomplish their work. In either case, workers "muddle through" the stages in the work process making alterations and refinements as they go. An envisioned product, idea, or service may emerge quite different from its original conception. In concluding, we will point out some of the implications of this work process model.

First, this model provides strategic intervention locations for improving the efficiency of work activity and for the enhancement of personal satisfaction for workers. Much could be learned by scrutinizing the various stages in the work process sequence for all varieties of work. Improvements could result from better understanding.

Second, it may be useful to employ this model to better understand and perhaps reduce many of the mistakes that occur in the work place. If workers "muddle through" their work activities, errors can result from simple miscalculations or deficiencies in social organization (Riemer, 1976). These errors can be costly to consumers. Locating exactly where these errors arise in the work sequence may provide the knowledge needed for their elimination.

Third, this model may provide additional insight into worker alienation. If a worker is limited in the control he or she has over the stages in the work process sequence, does this not lead to feelings of powerlessness, meaninglessness, social isolation, and self estrangement (Blauner, 1964; Israel, 1971)? And aren't workers who have maximum control over the stages in the work process sequence the least alienated (Work In America, 1973)?

Fourth, this model provides insight into the importance of the internalization phase in the work process sequence. We have too often ignored that thinking about how one is going to do a job is a critical element in getting that work completed. If we don't

31

see certain workers sweating and toiling we often think they are not working.

Fifth, this model could shed light on another neglected area of study – team work. When workers share a task, how does this influence the work process? Would matching team members according to abilities affect how they move through the work process sequence?

Sixth, this model may provide some important insights at the theoretical level. Would we expect workers who have maximum control over the entire work process sequence (such as fine artists) to show more or less variation in their completed products than workers who have less control?

The work process is highly social. Various work procedures may facilitate self-expression, provide association with others, create problems and stress, and produce social identity. Doing work in a particular way has consequences for workers and society. By drawing from environmental resources, manipulating these stimuli, and presenting the results to others, workers reflect and affect their social environment. We hope that the model presented here and the questions raised will provide the necessary stimulus for continued research in this area.

YES, BUT IS IT "ART"? - ARTISTS' VALUES

Like other occupational groups, artists share
understandings and atttitudes about their work. Art
and art work can be evaluated from the perspectives
of autonomous, inner-directed, or other-directed
value orientations. These orientations will influence artists' standards for good art and their expression of personal values in art work. This chapter reports research findings describing artists'
evaluations of art and art work. Shared orientations are presented for artists as an occupational
group and for the sub-groupings of fine artists,
amateur artists, art educators, and design artists.

Previous research places artists' occupational values in a social context. Artists do not work
in a vacuum; they are guided by the standards of
their occupation, like other occupational groups.
Krause (1971) compared the work of scientists and
artists, finding many similarities in the creative
nature and intense personal involvement of their
work. According to Griff (1964) and Strauss (1970),
many occupational values are formulated during the
recruitment and training process. Even after artists achieve success, they rely upon the involvement and evaluation of their peers and perceptive
audiences to reinforce their standards (Rosenberg
and Fliegel, 1965:203). Describing the essential
elements of artists' occupational values is the
purpose of this chapter. What are artists' standards for good art? What do artists strive to
achieve in their work?

ARTISTS' VALUE ORIENTATIONS

The concepts of autonomy, inner-directedness,
and other-directedness are appropriate for delin-
eating occupational values (Riesman, 1961:111,
1968:457). Each concept provides a pattern of
work orientation by outlining workers' attitudes
toward their work, themselves, and others. Members of the same occupational group will tend to

share attitudes toward work skills, standards of evaluation, and personal involvement in work. Riesman's concepts will help to construct the occupational value orientation of artists. Following Riesman's lead, these conceptual definitions will be used:

Autonomous Value Orientation

The outstanding characteristic of autonomy is a high level of self-awareness coupled with respect for one's own feelings and capabilities. Autonomously formulated values can transcend "adjusted" attitudes (Riesman, 1961: 243) because personal judgments are developed through intense personal involvement, not by acceptance of prevailing standards. A spirit of questioning, testing, and individuality permeates autonomy.

Inner-Directed Value Orientation

The values of inner-direction stress the quality of work being done. Emphasis on skill is reinforced by commitment to specific goals. These goals are individually chosen but fall within the range of possibilities which were established in childhood (or in occupational training). Craftsmanship directed by an "inner gyroscope" of principles constitutes an inner-directed value structure.

Other-Directed Value Orientation

Participation in communication is a highly valued other-directed characteristic. Sensitivity to others and a willingness to accept the judgment of others (Riesman, 1961: 138) underlies the cosmopolitan nature of other-directed attitudes. Because other-directed values are selected by "radar" from others, flexibility is a necessary trait of this type.

Others have studied the relationship between these concepts and artistic involvement. When she applied Riesman's character types to college students, Sofer (1961) found that the group aspiring to unconventional occupations (such as art) tended to have autonomous characteristics. This group resisted conformity and had strong, self-accepting self-images. The association of artistic interest with expressive roles and the artist's sensitivity to personal values has been studied by Kavolis (1963) and Merrill (1968). In her study of working artists Roe (1946) found that successful artists were capable of transcending environments, drawing from personal stimuli, and losing themselves in their work.

These works suggest that the value orientations of artists will be self-directed. Thus, Riesman's autonomous and inner-directed concepts are likely to describe many aspects of the artistic value orientation. However, there may be an emphasis on one of these value orientations over the other, or there may be some tendencies toward the other-directed orientation. Bell (1961:403) has expressed concern that the personal aspect of art work has been diminished by an other-directed society.

The following research findings will present attitudes of artists toward art and art work. There is a likelihood that self-directed attitudes will prevail for the entire group, but there are likely to be specific occupational differences among fine artists, amateur artists, art educators, and design artists.

DEFINING GOOD ART

The criteria used by artists to define "good art" reflect their values concerning art. By employing personal judgments, traditional aesthetic standards, or reflections of others' opinions to evaluate art, artists reveal their fundamental approach to art work. Is the goal of art self-awareness, exercise of skill, or communication with others? The means of evaluating art thus reveals autonomous, inner-directed, or other-directed orientations and can be used to characterize artists as a group or to compare sub-groupings of artists.

Artists were asked to respond to the question "How would you define good art?" Each written response was interpreted holistically according to its total meaning. In the few cases where a single chief idea did not emerge, the first idea was coded as that artist's response. Each artist's response was then coded as autonomous, inner-directed, or other-directed.

Evaluation Criteria

Autonomous Value Orientation

Responses which indicated autonomous values emphasized self-awareness and sensitivity to the artist's expression. Autonomous criteria require good art to be stimulating, creative, and spontaneous. Personal judgment is employed in evaluating these features. A special feeling about the art is sought,--or as one fine artist put it, "zat little somesing." (122) Many artists simply stated that art is good if they like it. However, one art educator was more direct, replying, "What I do is good art." (142)

Evaluating art autonomously calls for recognition and respect for one's feelings and judgments. Thus several artists reported that their definitions of good art changed as they developed their own art skills. Emphasizing a subjective response does not imply that there are as many levels of art as there are people, but requires each viewer to choose criteria based on self-knowledge. Art is good if it stimulates self-awareness. As one fine artist put it, "Does it move me? Do I feel something? Does it tickle me (make my imagination stand on its tip-toes)?" (173)

Inner-Directed Value Orientation

The criteria which indicate inner-directed evaluations of art are craftsmanship and adherence to principles. An art educator stated that "too much sloppy work is being done by would-be artist-craftsmen who have had little or no training..." (002) and this work would not meet inner-directed standards. Balance, order, and design are aspects of art which show adherence to accepted standards. Knowledge of artistic principles is necessary for creating good art.

Good art also demonstrates ethical qualities.

36

The principles of honesty, integrity, and sincerity are appreciated. Many artists expressed deep
feelings about this aspect of art and punctuated
their comments with exclamation marks. For example, an amateur artist defined good art as work
which is "...real and genuine and shows no form of
fraud!!" (120) Good art will not be phoney, gim-
micky, deceitful, superficial, or done only for
shock value. Good art is an honorable piece of
craftsmanship. Inner-directed artists require
sincerity as an expression of serious intent and
hard work.

Other-Directed Value Orientation

Other-directed standards require that art
participate in the circulation of ideas. Good art
is valued for its ability to communicate statements or meanings. For one design artist good art
is simply "instant and unmistakable communication." (076) For others, good art must be relative to the times since it is a medium which at-
tracts viewers and reflects their perceptions of
art. It is "something that satisfies everyone--
amateur, professional, critic, (062) according to
one amateur artist. Sometimes the audience is
more limited, however. For design artists artistic standards may be provided by an employer, a
client, or the demands of the job. Here good art
is whatever is marketable and serves a purpose.

Other-directed standards of art, then, are
relative. Goodness of art varies with its ability
to communicate with and be accepted by viewers.
The design artist who wrote, "One man's ceiling is
another man's floor," (162) was summarizing the
cosmopolitan perspective that standards for judg-
ing art are dependent upon the needs and reactions
of viewers. Art is useful as a tool for reaching
others.

FINDINGS

The artists as a group reported using autonomous
criteria more (39%) than inner-directed criteria (37%)
or other-directed criteria (24%) to define good art.
This finding is appropriate for an occupational group
whose products are expressive and creative. This finding also demonstrates that art is not evaluated only by

37

TABLE 1

EVALUATION CRITERIA, BY TYPE OF ARTIST

	Fine Artist	Amateur Artist	Art Educator	Design Artist
	% (N=22)	% (N=15)	% (N=35)	% (N=26)
Autonomous	47	42	36	31
Inner-Directed	39	41	45	24
Other-Directed	14	17	19	45
Total	100	100	100	100

personal standards; artists also judge the craftsmanship and communicative qualities of art. The findings
for the four types of artists are shown in Table 1.

Fine artists were more likely (47%) to utilize
autonomous criteria than the other artists. This group
of artists is most oriented toward the feeling aspect
of art, but amateur artists utilize autonomous criteria
nearly as often (42%). There is a clear definition between these two groups and the art educators and design
artists who utilize autonomous criteria less often
(thirty-six percent and thirty-one percent, respective-
ly).

Inner-directed criteria were most often used by
art educators (45%), although amateur artists (41%) and
fine artists (39%) were also quite likely to judge art
by its craftsmanship and adherence to principles. These
groups show an interest in the "doing" of art which is
not shared by as many design artists. Only twenty-four
percent of the design artists reported using inner-directed criteria.

Other-directed criteria are used by forty-five percent of the design artists to define good art. Other
groups do not report similar interest in art as a form
of communication. Nineteen percent of the art educators, seventeen percent of the amateur artists, and
only fourteen percent of the fine artists reported using other-directed criteria to define good art.

These findings show variation in the values employed by artists to define good art. The autonomous
criteria most frequently used by fine artists reflect
an orientation toward art which is based upon individual
feelings. An inner-directed value-orientation expressed
through emphasis on craftsmanship is appropriate to art
educators. These standards are in keeping with their
teaching of the skills and principles of art. The other-directed orientation reported most often by design
artists manifests suitable standards for those who produce art for a market and for a function.

Although the responses of amateur artists do not
display a primary value orientation, their interests
are similar to both fine artists and art educators. As
hobbyists, amateur artists appreciate the feeling aspects of art, and as amateurs they are concerned about
the techniques and accepted standards of art.

PERSONAL INVOLVEMENT IN ART

Because artists have sometimes been viewed as special messengers of values and ideas, art appreciators may search art for expressions of personal or social comment. To what extent do artists perceive themselves in this role?

The artists in this study were asked, "Which of your personal values are reflected in your art work?" The written replies were coded holistically as indicating autonomous, inner-directed, or other-directed characteristics. Each artist's reply was coded as one of these types.

Value Orientation

Autonomous Value Orientation

The essential characteristic of autonomous responses was self-awareness. These responses indicated that artists attempt to express their inner selves through art. For example, a fine artist wrote, "My art is me!" (129) These artists wished to express an original perspective of life, nature, and other people. Striving to project "...a vision of objects, animals, people, etc., as they are and not as we might like to think they are" (046) is an autonomous attempt to transcend the accepted point of view. These artists consciously attempt to develop a uniquely sensitive expression of their value. The work of a ceramicist reflects "...an earthy, liberal, spontaneous, and sensitive character. It is rough and organic, not precise and organized." (052)

Inner-Directed Value Orientation

Artists expressing inner-directed characteristics indicated that their personal values were of great importance. They felt that these standards directed their art work. "There is no amoral artist," (100) stated one art educator, and several design artists indicated that personal standards determined which assignments they would accept.

Discipline, honesty, and hard work were values these artists sought to express in their art work, as well as good technique and "...perfec-

40

tion in small detail." (144) Working according to the standards of art itself is important to these artists. The "hardness of the material" (Riesman, 1961:111) compels these artists to express order, balance, and harmony through the discipline of art.

Other-Directed Value Orientation

Artists who reported that communicating with others or using art to fulfill a function were the values likely to be reflected in their art work were categorized as other-directed. For them, accomplishment of a purpose is more important than self-expression, craftsmanship, or making statements about deep convictions. They value the consequences of art above the process of art work.

The comments of these artists showed that they value the responses of others (peers, public, or clients) and they are sensitive to current viewer demands. One amateur artist wrote, "I try to do things that are relevant to today." (024) For some this is a matter of eliciting emotions from viewers or an attempt to awaken awareness.

> "The conscious part of my art involves breaking people's preconceived ideas about art. I want to hit a repressed feeling level." (009)

Some artists indicated their art would be of little value if it did not arouse emotions in viewers.

For design artists others' responses are valued in more concrete ways. When design artists fill assignments they must be aware of the clients' schedules, pocketbooks, and tastes. Any reflection of personal values is often secondary to these contingencies. As one artist put it, "Being in the commercial end of art, I am rarely at liberty to interject my personal values into the work." (076) But design artists are not necessarily trapped by the needs of clients; some reported refusing assignments which infringed on their values. Others emphasized tolerance for others' values, as did this design artist: "I have not tried to educate the public. I am a Republican and a Congregationalist. Each for his own!!!" (061) Such a statement may either indicate a sensitive cosmopolitan or a glad-handed lack of standards.

Either way, it is an expression of other-direction.

Findings

Table 2 presents the findings on the reflection of artists' values in their work. Fifty percent of the artists expressed an autonomous orientation. The inner-directed orientation was expressed by 34% and the other-directed by 16%.

The most frequent autonomous response was given by amateur artists at 67%. Doing art for the purpose of expressing feelings and viewpoints is compatible with a hobbyist approach. But almost 60% of the fine artists gave autonomous responses also, indicating a self-oriented definition of art work. Art educators place less value on the autonomous aspect of art work, yet 48% of them do express these values in their art work. Design artists were least likely, 35%, to report an autonomous reflection of values in their art work; this finding is compatible with the nature of their purposeful work.

The group most likely to utilize an inner-directed orientation toward personal values was the art educators. In teaching art the principles of art and ethics must frequently be put to use. Fine artists also indicate a moderate tendency toward the inner-directed orientation (41%). The qualities of skill and discipline are less likely to be reflected in the work of design artists (27%) and amateur artists (13%).

In contrast, other-directed qualities are most likely to be reported by design artists (39%) and amateur artists (20%). This orientation toward communication with others is not shared by art educators (9%) or fine artists (0%). Reflecting one's personal values in an other-directed way is least likely to occur in art work.

These findings show that artists as a group value self-expression in their art work more than they value the consequences of art. But this pattern varies. Fine artists emphasize the autonomous aspects of art and ignore the other-directed. Amateur artists are highly autonomous but are also somewhat other-directed. For art educators, both inner-directed and autonomous values are important. Design artists show a completely different pattern, emphasizing the other-directed but also

42

TABLE 2

VALUES REFLECTED IN ART WORK, BY TYPE OF ARTIST

	Fine Artist	Amateur Artist	Art Edu-cator	Design Artist
	% (N=22)	% (N=15)	% (N=35)	% (N=26)
Autonomous	59	67	48	35
Inner-Directed	41	13	43	27
Other-Directed	0	20	9	38
Total	100	100	100	100

indicating that inner-directed and autonomous values are reflected in their work.

DISCUSSION

A pattern of value orientations has been found in artists' definitions of good art and the expression of artists' values in art work. This pattern shows a primarily autonomous orientation with strong inner-directed influence. Other-directed orientations are least frequently reported.

Figure 1 shows the ranking of each artist group on the two measures of value orientations. Rank 1 indicates the highest percent; rank 4, the lowest. When the two rankings of each artist group are compared on autonomous, inner-directed, and other-directed orientations, definite patterns emerge.

In the autonomous orientation, fine artists and amateur artists ranked second and first, art educators ranked third on both measures, and design artists ranked fourth on both measures.

For the inner-directed orientation, art educators rank first on both measures, fine artists second and third, design artists third and fourth, and amateur artists have split rankings of second and fourth.

The other-directed orientation shows more clear patterns. Design artists rank first, fine artists rank fourth, and the amateur artists and art educators each hold one second and one third ranking for the two measures.

These combined rankings indicate differences in each group's understanding of art. Fine artists emphasize self-expressive values first and next skill-oriented values; they are least likely to see art as a means to an end. Art educators emphasize the skill aspects of art first, then its purposefulness and some degree of expressiveness. Design artists see art first as a purpose, and least in its expressive aspects.

For amateur artists there is a mixed approach. They are highly oriented to the expressive aspects of art, they have a moderate interest in the purposeful aspect and show mixed emphasis on the craftsmanship of art. Differences between groups are clearest between

44

FIGURE 1

ARTISTS' RANKINGS ON VALUE ORIENTATIONS*

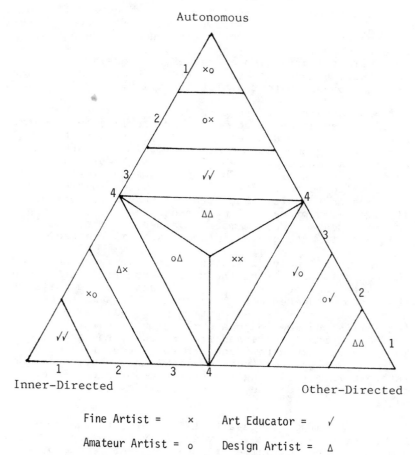

Fine Artist = ×   Art Educator = √

Amateur Artist = o   Design Artist = Δ

* 1 = highest percent,   4 = lowest percent

fine artists and design artists, but no group is found solely at the extremes of each measure.

The findings of this study show that artists share understandings of their work both as an entire group and as occupational sub-groupings. The values of autonomy and inner-directedness are strongly supported by artists. These are appropriate to the creative nature of art work, work which demands an investment of self. This point is also valid for design artists as only a minority expressed other-directed values on either measure.

Differences between the groups indicate different perceptions of art work arising from differences in selection, training, and work experience. Fine artists tend to express self-oriented values, art educators often reflect craft-oriented values, and design artists are likely to express result-oriented values. The value orientation of amateur artists is mixed.

Our data tend to support Durkheim's contention that an occupational group is characterized by a "moral power" which subordinates individual interests to the goal of the group (Durkheim, 1961:356). Artists tend to share autonomous value orientations moderated by inner-directed values. Sharing values should increase the likelihood that artists will work toward artistic, not personal, goals. But both of these value orientations are individual-oriented and appear antithetical to group goals. When members' values are individualistic, how will the group's standards be maintained?

Artists' individualistic values are functional for an occupation requiring innovation and originality. In this case the interests of individuals are the goals of the group. Adherence to autonomous values meets many needs of the artists' occupation. But values supporting skills and knowledge are also functional for meeting occupational goals and are valued by the group. Because artists share a concern for the quality of art work (as well as for individuality) they share a common interest in maintaining the standards of art. Inner-directed values define the acceptable range of individuality.

Our findings suggest that fine artists contribute to occupational standards by actively following the group's autonomous value orientation. Art educators' contribution arises from their transmission of shared skills and knowledge. Although amateur artists show relatively low interest in craftsmanship, they show a high regard for autonomy. Their low interest in skills and principles shows a lack of occupational socialization. Design artists are marginal members of the group. Their values tend to reflect practical, non-artistic goals. Amateur artists and design artists are least likely to make substantial contributions to art as an expression of shared expectations held by this group.

Although an occupational group may be characterized by individualistic values, group goals can still be achieved. By tempering individual aims with a shared concern for quality, artists encourage creativity within acceptable boundaries.

V.

IN THEIR OWN WORDS

This chapter is devoted to the views of seven contemporary Mid-American artists. Each artist approaches their art work from a slightly different vantage point. Some work as design artists. Others teach art as well as do art work. A few are considered fine artists of the first quality, while others are breaking into the art world. These artists include:

BLACK BEAR BOSIN, late internationally recognized Indian artist.

One of Mr. Bosin's best-known works is the gigantic sculpture, The Keeper of the Plains, located in Wichita, Kansas. Mr. Bosin was primarily a painter and he had exhibited widely. Throughout his career he also maintained The Great Plains Studio where he managed commercial art work. He died on August 9, 1980.

DEE CONNETT, Associate Professor of Fine Arts, Friends University.

Ms. Connett works in several media and has exhibited extensively while continuing her university teaching and functions. One of her interests for art education is the developing of business skills as they relate to art work.

ROBERT KISKADDEN, Assistant Dean, College of Fine Arts, Wichita State University.

Dean Kiskadden has a well-established career in water color and oil painting which he has developed in conjunction with college level teaching and administration. He is active in community art groups such as the Wichita Art Museum and the Wichita Artists Guild.

PAULA KREKOVICH, design artist.

Ms. Krekovich works in the design division of a greeting card company. She creates illustrations for various paper products. She also has management responsibilities over a group of supervisors of artists and is responsible for their work.

CHARLES SANDERSON, well-known Kansas watercolorist.

Mr. Sanderson has combined his own successful art work with teaching high school art students. In addition he has contributed to the development of Kansas artist groups such as the Kansas Watercolor Society and Group II.

NICK VACCARO, Professor of painting and sculpture, University of Kansas.

Mr. Vaccaro has been teaching at the college level since 1960. He has also been producing paintings which are exhibited at the national and international levels. Several of his works have won purchase awards.

FRAN WAGNER, amateur artist and student of the Wichita Art Association.

Ms. Wagner continues studying and producing oil paintings while also managing a household. She shows her work in the Wichita Art Association exhibits and sales gallery and expects to continue her art work as a personal goal.

The artists speak for themselves in this chapter on selected topics. Our decision to include certain comments in this section was based primarily on selecting content which could help other artists and art students to better understand their own situation. The verbatim comments that follow are taken from longer interviews conducted with these artists.

VACCARO: Advice to Students

We have a lot of students who idealistically have the romantic notion of being an artist and they get their degree in studio art. (They) go out and find that the most they can find is a commercial art job that pays the same whether they have a degree in art or not. They could get the same job with a high school education.

Some students with a B.F.A. (Bachelor of Fine Arts Degree) in art or design get out in the real world and discover that public schools won't hire them, junior colleges won't hire them, without a teaching certificate. So they come back and work strictly in the School of Education to take courses required for teaching certification. If they had known when they started college that they wanted to be an artist-teacher, they

could have double majored and earned both the studio
degree and the teaching certificate in four years.

Many people are confused concerning their preparation
for college teaching. I know I was. I started in art
education because I wanted to be a teacher. I didn't
know that one didn't have to have an Art Education degree and a teaching certificate if they wanted to teach
studio art at the college or university level. . . . If
you are a studio oriented person, the thing to do is
get an undergraduate degree and a Master's degree in
the specific area that you want to teach. We hire people who have a Master of Fine Arts Degree. We don't
care if they ever taught in a public school or anywhere
for that matter. We hire on the basis of their art
work primarily and the recommendations from people they
have studied with. We look very scantily at transcripts
and things like that. We are more concerned about the
quality of their art work.

SANDERSON: On Learning the Basics

Students . . . have to visualize, they have to think,
they have to learn. Like watercolor, you have to know
what a brush will do, what the paint will do, what the
paper will do. One hundred and forty pound paper is
different from two hundred or three hundred. Water
color board is different. Each paint is different.
If you buy a new brush, it is different from the old
one. There is different spring in the brush. The
paper changes; the quality of the paper changes. It
is never the same. I make paper changes all of the
time. You may have one idea and it works great. You
have to remember these things. The humidity affects
these things. Drying time - it is different painting
in the Winter time than in the Fall, Summer, or Spring.
You have to remember these things. It is a long process of finding out. When you touch a brush to a paper,
what is going to happen? If you use a wet on wet technique, what is going to happen to that paint? (Students) need to experiment with paint to see how it
flows. Find the fascinating things that will develop
right in front of you. You get this backlog of things
in your mind of what to do next. Sometimes you forget
it. I cannot paint two of the same thing; there is no
way.

KISKADDEN: On the Importance of Training

It is really not enough that people have talent or express or exhibit a kind of talent. Many people in adult
education do not understand this. They think, "Now, I
would like to paint," but they have no structure on
which to base this idea. It is true you can paint,
but a struggle emerges. Without the training it is
more apt to have disastrous results. They have all
the excitement, all the energy, the drive, and pretty
soon their work bogs down. It bogs down in most cases
because they don't have the training behind them to
carry through. In education, I call it "carry-over."
One may have some training in a variety of areas.
Everyone does. You begin by placing more and more
information together and this trained information carries you through to the next plateau. When one has
the aptitude plus the training, rigorous or not, you
develop a freedom of choice. A good freedom of choice
is always backed by training.

SANDERSON: On Good Students

In just a few days I can tell whether they have talent
(by) watching how they absorb what you are saying.
Take the talented one, you can talk to them, they understand you. They may do a drawing and you say that
is a good idea, let's go on from there, (or) try this
technique or this medium. The good student (is the
one) who looks interested and you can tell them how to
do something and they will try it. They may get frus-
trated but if you keep encouraging them they will go
on. Then there is the other student who does not give
a hang. (For them), art is nothing. (They say), I
don't have to think. I don't like your ideas. You
want what you like, and I say no that is not it. We
are talking about design, what you can do with a simple
line, what you can develop.

CONNETT: On the Basics

Technique, craftsmanship, and good quality design (are
basic). . . . Design is the backbone of all art, whether
it is three dimensional or two dimensional. Design is
the most important thing. That is part of the academic
training of art and some people have a much better design quality in their work than others. Craftsmanship
is important too. Is the thing going to last?

You have to know the basics before you can destroy
them. A lot of people do not understand that in the
abstraction of art. Oh, my little two year old could
do that, or any chimpanzee could do that. But they do
that by accident if they get good design. You need
to know the basics before you can start taking liber-
ties.

KREKOVICH: On Training

It all depends on what you want in the end. I've done
some college recruiting and I find that people from
art schools tend to want to be artists for the rest of
their days. They want to be a known illustrator, a
known package designer or whatever. But people who
come from a university want to go into management. I
suppose that is a glaring generalization but it seems
to be that way, possibly because people at the university have a broader range (of education).

If you think that art work is what you want to do the
rest of your life, if that is the ultimate goal in
your life - to be the best in your field, then I would
recommend that people be trained in an art school,
where they get a finer training and not just a broad
education.

SANDERSON: Advice to Students

You have to know business and you have to be able to
correspond. . . . You need a business course, you need
language arts courses, you have to be able to communicate. I like to talk about art but I am not a great
speaker. You have to impress people. You have to impress them personally - your work is not enough.

CONNETT: On Teaching

I do not work myself during the class time with the
students. I may bring things in and show them an example of what I am trying to get them to work toward
or something like that. They have seen my work most
of the time in progress. But as far as working right
in the studio with the students, I do not.

I think (it helps the students). I do not want a bunch
of little stereotypes coming out of the studio that

53

paint like me. I have seen a lot of schools that you can tell exactly which school the student went to or which teacher they had when they studied there. I do not like that idea, it is kind of against my philosophy. I try to get them to think for themselves and experiment rather than copy what I do. . . . Plus, I think they are paying me to teach them not for me to do my work here.

SANDERSON: On Discipline

I found a lot of students have to learn the hard way. There is a point when you are working on a painting or an art form and you have to have self discipline. You get to a point where you need to quit. So many times students quit because they don't think they are going anywhere. . . . it's not working. You can have an idea in mind - but, you put it on paper but it doesn't work. I had to force myself to go on and solve my problems. I found out that there is always a solution if you keep looking long enough. I kept looking and of course I teach during the day and I would force myself to come down here (his home studio) every night and work. I have to do this now because it is just part of me. It is not work. I enjoy painting and I don't just to be successful. . . I think it is exciting - I can do something I can enjoy and other people want to buy. I think it's really great.

KISKADDEN: On Art History

Most people are unwilling to study the history of art for a general background. We insist at the university that you have a general background in order to know what man has accomplished. If you aren't exposed, you really don't know. You will not have a vocabulary to do anything. Your system of judgment will be limited. Knowing how to compare is helpful. This is also part of your training. The two systems placed side by side aid you considerably in the creative process.

BOSIN: On Indian Artists

Some of us. . . are reaching back into time. We are idealistic, I suppose, envisioning a world that once was and certainly we are making it a lot more palatable, adding a lot more beauty to it and it is all in

54

our mind. But then where else would it be.

VACCARO: On Good Art

The only art that is important to me is the kind of art
that once I see it, I'm no longer the same person I
used to be. I'm talking about great art, not good art.
Good art is prevalent; there is a lot of good art a-
round. I'm talking about that category of art that
changes your life. It no longer lets you be the same
person you used to be. It enlarges you. That is the
most meaningful art. It doesn't have to be from today;
it can be from 300 years ago or 3,000 years ago. It
has to be something that when you encounter it, you
know it. But it is not like a knowledge kind of knowing; it is knowing without knowledge. . . . Art is a
matter of opinion.

CONNETT: On Good Art

Sometimes you have a good feeling about it and sometimes you are not your best judge. I like to have
people who are not in the art area to judge me because
then you get kind of the public reaction. I guess you
could call it a gut reaction to your art. . . . It is
really a game of chance because you are never sure what
a juror is going to like.

SANDERSON: On Good Art

Good art is when the artist shows he knows his technique, like the surface he is working on, his subject
matter, does he have control of the medium, does he
have good content.

WAGNER: On Good Art

The first thing would be integrity. It has to not only
promise, but deliver. It has to be something you can
live with year after year and always feel fresh about.
. . . It is always contributing.

Bosin: On Struggling for Achievement

I think all creative people are going to do this no

55

matter what. It is an adversity, certainly. The only
thing to do is new. It is not going to be easy from
that point on because you have to constantly produce in
order to satisfy that inner ego you have. And always
the next picture is going to be your best one and it
never is. You can always see improvement. I think artists were given a certain amount of paintings to do in
their particular life. When they do that they are gone.
A kind of fatalistic type thing, I suppose.

CONNETT: How to Build a Reputation

Work. Start off by entering shows. People do not understand that sometimes. Competitive shows are quite
different from art fairs. At art fairs people buy your
work because they like it and they hang it on the wall.
Sometimes you get little artsy, craftsy types of art
things - painted rocks and things like that. But in a
competitive art show you will have an art museum or
gallery that sends notices out and there will be several
judges. They may be directors of art museums, art historians, or well known in their various areas. . . .
Most shows are judged by slides. You send slides of
your work, they flash them on a screen, it is thumbs up
or thumbs down. . . . They keep weeding these out. . . .
(You may be) fortunate enough to just get into the show,
then if you happen to get a purchase award or patrons
award or some kind of prize above that that even makes
it better.

It is kind of like developing a pedigree. I have compared it to a dog show. You are the dog and if you get
enough blue ribbons, that makes you a master.

It is expensive. They have entry fees. You have to
pay anywhere from $5.00 to $10.00 per entry with a maximum of say from 3 to 5 entries. Then if your slide is
accepted, you pay the expense of the postage to get it
there and insurance. They are not responsible for anything happening to your work. . . . And it is competitive. There are more and more artists all the time.

VACCARO: On Establishing a Reputation

There appears to be two different ways that most artists have gained recognition, at least in this country.
One of them is through competitive exhibitions plus one
person exhibitions and invitational exhibitions. There

are (also) artists who never send to competitions. (They) are either invited by showing a portfolio of work to a gallery director or their friends point out their work to gallery directors. There are numerous artists who have never entered the competitive art world. By this, I mean open competition, where you submit work and it is juried and the work is selected for awards and inclusion, or rejected.

SANDERSON: On Developing a Reputation

For myself, I started in art fairs. (The student should try) to make one or two good contacts. A gallery saw my work and asked me to exhibit. What it boils down to is you have to take your work out. You cannot leave your work in the studio and expect the public to come to you - they won't. It is competitive. There are very few people who understand what the artist is trying to do. Most of them want to buy something so the color matches their drapes. It is very frustrating. When someone comes here looking for a painting for their drapes, I leave, I can't take it.

WAGNER: On Developing a Reputation

A lot of it is luck. Some of it is not deserved while some of it is richly deserved. There are some artists who are obviously great there is no denying it. But, I think, a lot of people who are trying are not all that good.

(This happens) because the public does not have an excellent taste in art. Sometimes their judgment is based on nostalgia or bright colors or whatever they happen to like. Art is very personal. Sometimes one strong point will make a person sell while somebody else who is doing overall better work is not as popular.

KREKOVICH: On Establishing a Reputation

I think probably the big thing is to get a foothold somewhere. Go into the greeting card business or go into an agency or into a studio and do all the (routine) work for several years. Eventually, build up so that you are doing some of the original work (that will lead to) a reputation. It takes a good deal of time.

BOSIN: On the Pitfalls of Recognition

It is a matter of getting up to this particular plateau in art and then being recognized as some kind of
authority when all I want to do is paint. But I'm
asked to lecture and all things that are completely
arbitrary to my lifestyle that I try to maintain. Then
to be dubbed these kind of names and to have to react
to them in order to maintain some kind of continuity
with the viewing public and the people who really need
to know, and I know they need to know (about Indian
art). I do not paint with the abandon that I used to
because of this. All of a sudden I am supposed to be
one of the old masters as somebody called me. That
does not set well with me because that means everything
I do is going to be examined minutely. I do not want
my things to be examined like that. . . . This is one
of the crosses, I guess, that is supposed to be borne
at this particular time. It is not a happy combination.
. . . All too often, in these times, and I suppose clear
back into past times, you can find people who are buying the name rather than the artist. So, the artist
has to maintain a quality that is beyond question each
and every time.

CONNETT: On Black Periods

People get into depressions. I have noticed that a lot
of artists go through a black period. They will paint
in dark colors. I have got to the point that I recog-
nize when I am going into one of my depression periods
and I will fight it out. I start painting in brighter
colors.

BOSIN: On Dry Periods

It is a very strange thing. It has happened to me
several times. The worst dry spell, I suppose, was
several years back. I think I went 3 or 4 years without painting. But I've had those things before, for
weeks or months at a time. A strange thing happens
during that interim, I have never been able to fathom,
nor have I thought about it too much or talked about it
too much. During those particular periods, I want to
paint, I want to create, very badly. But that is not
the only stimulus. There is something else besides that
that I have never been able to fathom.

The well is full, but I can't get the bucket down to it.
Then all of a sudden, I don't know what it is -- I suppose it is like the bear who hibernates. The scientists
have yet to figure out what the stimulus is to make him
ultimately seek his den for the winter. They have
watched them, day after day through all kinds of snows,
winds blowing, they are practically asleep on their
feet, and then at a certain moment they all go. I suppose that is the way I am. At a certain moment, I do
it.

It is very, very frustrating. I try to stimulate myself by buying brushes, by buying paints, paper, board,
canvases, buying books, travel, look, look, and watch.
I seek (other artists) out and become very inspired
while talking to them. I walk 5 steps away from them
and it is gone. Very strange.

I swear to God I am going to keep it up (painting).
Yet, I always finish a painting and I have to stop and
that is when it happens sometimes. Rarely, in the
middle of a painting.

VI.

FINDING SPACE IN THE GALLERY - EPILOGUE

Being an artist is becoming increasingly compli-
cated as the artist and the public move toward closer
association. The art boom which began in the U.S.
during the late 1950's has cracked the protective wall
around the artist's world, intensifying the ambiguities
of the artist's social position. Having experienced
extreme alienation in the past while serving as models
of "elevated consciousness", artists now discover that
recent changes in society both increase sources of alienation and also present opportunities for developing
a new social role. (Ackerman, 1969; Griff, 1959; Rosenberg and Fliegel, 1965).

Artists today confront a complex challenge: how
can they continue to sustain artistic values while the
public attempts to smother them with an insatiable desire for artistic products? Common man has discovered
art (Elkhoff, 1970; Poggioli, 1970).

With this narrowing of social distance between
artists and consumers new relationships have developed.
Old images of "philistine" consumers and "bohemian"
artists interfere with today's market conditions. The
modern artist is faced with a new social situation, one
based upon role integration rather than role exclusion.
In this chapter we describe the social conditions that
have encouraged alienation and introduce a new role
which artists are beginning to construct in response
to a changing social environment.

THE SOCIAL POSITION OF ARTISTS

Historical hindsight allows us to see that the
social position of artists has been altered before.
The artist as craftsman (guild-member) of the Middle
Ages was replaced by the Academy-member artist of the
Renaissance. When this change occurred, artists were
removed from the mundane world. The more renowned at-
tained positions as learned men, becoming closely associated with the upper levels of political and religious groups. Patronage became the foundation of
relationships between artists and collectors, and the
artist's image became that of creative genius (Bell,
1970; Pelles, 1963).

61

In the late 19th century the system of formal a-
cademies and rigid definitions of art gave way before
a growing population of artists and affluent bourgeois
consumers. The resulting strain on the older, more
limited system of academy-trained, patron-supported art
production shattered relationships between known collectors and artists. Artists began to sell their works
to a large unknown audience through dealers rather than
to known collectors (White, 1965). At the same time
many artists adopted a romantic ideology which separated them from their more materialistic middle-class
consumers (Griff, 1959). An image of artists developed
which portrayed them as rebels, madmen, starving her-
mits, people who spoke more easily with their muses
than with their families. Artists and their public
knew each other only from a distance.

Each of these changes in social position produced
greater social distance between artists and others.
Craftsmen-artists had face-to-face relationships with
customers of different social rank and were not considered to be a separate order of human being as were
the later Academy-member artists. While the Academy
artist did associate with social superiors, the artist's genius role effectively limited intimacy and pre-
vented most artists from holding influential social positions. Removing artists ideologically and socially
from others created the most extreme separation for the
bohemian artist, and for the last century, this has
been the typical social position of artists.

Setting artists apart from ordinary people through
differences in ideologies and life styles also removed
them from the mundane world of making a living. Dealers, critics, museum curators, collectors, and art
historians have served as liaisons between artists and
publics. In so doing they have protected artists from
many distractions inherent in ordinary life. But they
have also maintained the social distance between artists and others, contributing to the modern image of
the alienated artist and blocking channels for public
understanding.

ALIENATION AND THE ARTIST'S ROLE

Even now the romantic myth of the starving, immoral
artist confronts future artists (and parents of future
artists) reinforcing their alienation. During the last
100 years artists have typified "Alienated Man" (Pelles,

1963). Seeman (1969) has suggested a conceptualization of alienation which readily describes the artists' dilemma. Social isolation, powerlessness, normlessness, self-estrangement, and meaninglessness are characteristic of the artist's social position today.

Social isolation of artists encourages the ideology of artists' communities and insulates artists from worldly distractions. Withdrawal from the mundane world is consistent with artistic ideology since artists may wish to express intellectual differences through the maintenance of social distance. Physically isolated artist communities such as SoHo, Sausalito, and Taos symbolize possible alternatives to the real world, but social and intellectual distance between artist and public is not entirely practical or beneficial.

When artists wish to impart serious yet disturbing ideas from an isolated social position they may find few avenues of communication available to them. Isolation reinforces the public's image of the idiosyncratic artist and their ideas are considered frivolous (Kozloff, 1974). The public expects artists to dissent, artists expect to be condemned, and neither side attempts to comprehend the other. "Avant-gardisme is condemned to a liberty which is slavery, and to serve too often the negative and destructive principle of art for art's sake" (Poggioli, 1970:686).

The nature of artists' social position has rendered them powerless to affect the values of society or even to influence the evaluation of their own works. Art work is defined and evaluated by the market, not by creative standards. Producing works which are not well received by critics and dealers is tantamount to economic and emotional disaster. Being discovered posthumously has little effect on one's budget or need for appreciation. Although desire to communicate may be intense, the constricted roles and relationships available for dispensing intellectual products restrict the artist's ability to affect society.

By confining themselves to an idealistic art world artists encourage the manipulation of themselves and their art by the "Art Establishment" (Bell, 1970). Because artists accept an image of themselves as being morally pure and superior to materialistic motivations, they have accepted a powerless position. They foster the notion that they cannot cope with the practical financial aspects of life and that others must act in their behalf (Wayne, 1973). As a powerless group, artists are ineffective in controlling their own destiny.

Normlessness in the art world reinforces isolation and powerlessness. The public can play an important part in artistic processes by conscientiously considering the meaning and work of art products; by so doing they complete the communication initiated by artists and reinforce norms concerning art. But the public has become an undependable audience as it shifts its tastes more rapidly than ever before. The trend toward vogue rather than discrimination threatens existing standards for art, with innovation replacing creativity among artists concerned with public's cravings (Rosenberg and Fliegel, 1965). The market creates an ambiguous position for the artist because of the commercial value imposed upon art work (Mills, 1970). However, Harold Rosenberg (1970), an influential art critic, denies the effective functioning of an Art Establishment; he states that a few critics, dealers, and collectors cannot alone cause new art forms to succeed, but that the ultimate power returns to the artist. The fact that many artists strenuously disagree with this perception underscores the normlessness of the situation.

If society tends to accept any artistic innovation, what is the value of art work? Perhaps the answer lies in the incompatible expectations of public and artist. If the public does not comprehend art work nor react to it on the level intended by the artist, then the function of art is unfulfilled. The artist's role lacks meaning; "art for art's sake" is an insufficient justification for producing art. In response to this dilemma many artists substitute a nonconformist lifestyle for producing creative work (Wolfe, 1975). Rebelliousness and non-conformity are then honored and paid for by the public as recognition for the image of creativity (Bell, 1970). Giving meaning to the human condition through art, a classic function of artists, receives less attention than the appearance of being an artist.

Like other alienated workers, artists suffer from these condtions and become self-estranged. Being "other-directed" is a modern dilemma for artists. When older artists claim that younger artists are becoming organization men (Elkhoff, 1970) or that they are selling out to success (Rosenberg and Fliegel, 1965), they are noting the symptoms of a modern shift from "inner-directedness" to "other-directedness" which most other occupational groups have already undergone (Ackerman, 1969).

Suffering alienation is not exclusively an intellectual issue. For artists the issue is often one of physical survival; how <u>does</u> one make a living while creating art? The constant strain of being a symbol of non-materialism for society causes a sense of martyrdom and emphasizes the artists' eccentricities over the art itself. The art may suffer as artists are isolated from the full range of ordinary human experience and can only test ideas against a limited audience. But most importantly alienation of the artist reinforces the artist-elite relationship and gives the elite more control over the production of art while at the same time depriving a wider audience of the art experience. By submitting to alienation the artist plays into the hands of the elite. Goffman (1972:214) has noted that artists are one of the curator groups "whose task it is to build and service" the machinery of status. These groups manipulate symbols for a group to which they do not belong.

CHANGES IN THE ART WORLD

One might imagine that the recent proliferation of galleries, art education programs, museums and consumers, accompanied by rising prices and a broadening market, would have provided a solution to most of the artist's problems. There have been substantial improvements in the physical lives of artists who have succeeded financially, but other external factors have begun to exert themselves and are causing problematic changes in the entire art world. These changes are challenging artists to confront the materialistic world and at the same time maintain allegiance to the qualitative values of art.

After nearly two centuries of virtually ignoring the work of indigenous artists, American society has recently shown great interest in art as a commodity. Art is more likely now to be a profitable venture for more people than ever before. Elkhoff (1970) describes the American painter as a "Blue Chip," and observes that works of art are now traded, promoted, and publicized as any business commodity. To succeed now as a collector one must watch trends, diversify, merge interests, and so forth, in the manner of all investors. This sort of activity is, of course, antithetical to the aesthetic values of art itself. Burn (1975) observes that artists have been capitalized and marketed for an exchange market and states that this market is subject to manipulation by an elite.

Art products are increasingly being used as indicators of status achievement. Using art as a status symbol is old practice; what is new is the very large number of people employing the skills of artistic taste. The sale of art books, attendance at museum exhibitions, and the frequency of local art fairs all indicate a widespread interest in works of art. For the artist, the question is: what motivates this interest--acquisitiveness, status competition, a desire to decorate one's home, or an educated appreciation of the works purchased?

Another challenge to the artist comes from those institutions which have begun to support artists. The National Endowment for the Arts, the Business Committee for the Arts, and several large foundations have recently been making commitments to give substantial financial support to the visual arts. The relationship between business and art is intimate, although misunderstood. Business does not ignore the arts; rather, "... it is obvious that the businessman's product designers and advertising and promotion departments are parasitic on practically every art form" (Chagy, 1973:39). Business groups must support the visual arts since the work of creative artists stimulates the work of commercial designers. The fine artists are in a position to benefit from such interest if they are not disturbed by the motivation of their benefactors.

Due to the great volume of art being produced, the existing art distribution system does not function adequately. Myers surveyed the problems of New York contemporary artists in 1957 and found that there were too many artists in proportion to the number of galleries; that problem still exists (Chamberlain, 1970). Artists face problems in doing business with galleries and in having their works effectively reviewed. Older artists resent the promotion of young artists by dealers who are more often concerned with a new style than with a good one. Older artists also believe young artists "sell out" by perverting their work to suit a fashion. As one abstract expressionist commented, "I just don't understand this insidious, cynical way of looking at art as if there's a career in it" (Rosenberg and Fliegel, 1965:38). This generation gap in attitudes illustrates the new pressures imposed upon artists. New problems indicate change in the artist's role and possible sources for increased alienation. Due to the pressure of rising demand and increasing productivity the traditional expectations regarding the artist's social and economic function are being changed. A public having a higher standard of living, more leisure time, more travel experience, and more education is accustomed to having access to books and record albums and now they also want works of art. For artists, this demand constitutes a crisis, since traditional roles and organizations cannot adequately supply the market, nor has it been an expectation on the part of artists that they should supply a market.

EMERGENCE OF A NEW ROLE

Contending with alienation and dealing with social change is characteristic of modern life. There are alternatives to acceptance of these conditions, if one is aware of the forces which create such extensive influence over individuals. As Berger suggests (1963) society can be a stage inhabited by living actors just as it can be a puppet show or a prison. "Unlike the puppets, we have the possibility of stopping the machinery by which we have been moved" (Berger, 1963:176).

Roszack (1973:XXIV) describes the artist as one who most clearly perceives alienation and thus suffers most deeply; it is the arts which have produced the greatest number of "modern martyrs, persecuted prophets, and suffering saints." But embracing alienation is not life, only tragic illusion. Artists may enjoy certain benefits from an alienated condition, not the least of which is adulation from the public, but artists who understand the social nature of their condition may elect to change it.

Some artists are taking the initiative to resolve conflicts inherent in the artist's role. A new role is being constructed which emphasizes participation in society, not exclusion, and which minimizes myths (Sanders, 1976). As artists move toward more interaction with the public, their image becomes less elite, less isolated, and more independent of the Art Establishment. The artistic ideology which places art above the comprehension of laymen is being modified in favor of a more humanistic ideology. When art is viewed as one possible form of interaction among humans rather than as a product of alienated geniuses, the relationship between artist and the public becomes more direct. "Art for art's sake" loses support as the new artist's role opens more human possibilities to all. According to Anton (1968), the artist's new self-image emphasizes exploratory inward creative action in conjunction with intensive outward action that defends art against non-artistic demands. This new role grapples with the human dilemma of being a whole person among corrupting institutions and offers a model of an attempt to deal with alienation, rather than to suffer from it.

Since artists playing the new role are not acquiescing to those who manipulate art for inartistic purposes they are increasingly engaged in conflict. Meyer (1974) is optimistic that artists can acquire skills which will place them on a competitive level with dealers and purchasers. She describes the artist's "screwball image" (Meyer, 1974:6) as a self-fulfilling prophecy for those artists who isolate themselves from everyday business affairs; it is when artists accept that image that they become strange and impoverished.

Goodman (1974) advocates training artists in the skills of independent business in order to prevent artists from becoming passive and complaining about the world's ignorance of their work. Utilizing creative abilities to make art works available to an audience would not be an aesthetic sin within the new artist's role. Instead of renouncing business skills, artists can use them to serve the needs of the public and of themselves.

A similar mood can be found throughout the various artists' groups. One artists' publication with high circulation includes a "Professional Page" offering information on pricing, museum policies, and issues such as the "Projansky Agreement" which would provide artists a fifteen percent royalty on resale of their works. Since the militant years of the late 60's many of the more radical artists' groups dropped from sight, but the National Art Workers' Community still survives. Its functions now are quite pragmatic: providing employment services, insurance bargaining, and research into the economics of the art world (Skiles, 1975).

The mood of taking an initiative extends to art

68

educators and commercial artists. For those artists who live between New York and Los Angeles the best means of survival are in the university and college art departments, reports Potter (1973), but art educators at that level must continue to move forward artistically by encouraging the development of art centers, museums, and galleries in order to avoid the occupational hazard of security-by-tenure. Through the development of such facilities the regional audiences will be educated and artistically served at the same time that a distribution system is created for the artists.

Art educators at other levels of the educational systems are confronting professional problems by acquiring skills in budgeting, enrollment, and administration so that they will be prepared to defend and expand art programs (Mattil, 1971; Warwick, 1972). The trend in art education is to become more art conscious and less educationally conscious as illustrated by an experimental "Arts in General" program in the public schools which attempts to integrate art and education in all departments while emphasizing art as a subject. Such a program emphasizes the participatory nature of the new artist's role (Reiss, 1973). Commercial artists, too, are seeking to bridge the gap between traditional definitions of their work and their intentions to create a message for the public. Advertising agencies are giving more freedom to specialists in creative work (Cahn, 1971), some graphic artists are attempting to publicize the artistic value of their work (Upper & Lower Case, 1976), and some designers acknowledge a demand for more humanistic environments above the concern for materialistic and technological values (Design Quarterly, 1975).

Some artists would dispute the advantages of the new role. To them alienation provides known benefits. Because alienated artists have provided shocking new perceptions to society, they have played a "good deviant" role (Pelles, 1963:157) which many artists prefer. Recognition of the alienated artist as a martyr to the evils of materialistic society has been an additional source of social reinforcement. And problems are inherent in the new role. Loyalties may be divided between aesthetic and activist concerns, and public interest may be distracted from the artist's work to the artist's new social role.

But the alternative of remaining a puppet of soci-

69

ety will be difficult to choose as more artists achieve an understanding of that situation. Artists and their art need not be martyred for the sake of society. The new role for artists would allow artists to fulfill the imagery offered by Berger (1963): craftsmen-artists of the middle ages were prisoners in a social system; academy-member artists after the Renaissance were puppets for an elite; bohemian artists of the last century have been perceptive puppets who occasionally modified their performances; but the new artist will be an actor who must choose the way to play the artist's role.

REFERENCES

Ackerman, James S.
1969   "The Demise of the Avant-Garde: Notes on
            the Sociology of Recent American Art."
            Comparative Studies in Society and History
            11, 4 (October): 371-384.

Albrecht, M.C., J.H. Barnett and Mason Griff (eds.)
1970   The Sociology of Art and Literature: A
            Reader. New York: Praeger.

Anton, John P.
1968   "The Role and Dilemma of the Contemporary
            Artist." Buffalo Studies IV, 4 (December):
            71-106.

Barron, F.
1972   Artists in the Making. New York: Seminar
            Press.

Becker, H.S.
1960   "Notes on the Concept of Commitment." Am-
            erican Journal of Sociology 66: 32-40.

1974   "Art as Collective Action." American So-
            ciological Review 39: 767-776.

Becker, H.S. and Carper, J.W.
1956   "The Development of Identification with
            an Occupation." American Journal of Soci-
            ology 61: 289-298.

Becker, H.S. and Strauss, A.
1956   "Careers, Personality, and Adult Sociali-
            zation." American Journal of Sociology
            62: 253-263.

Bell, Quentin
1970   "Conformity and Nonconformity in the Fine
            Arts." In Milton D. Albrecht, James H.
            Barnett, and Mason Griff (eds.) The So-
            ciology of Art and Literature: A Reader.
            New York: Praeger, pp. 687-701.

Berger, Peter
1969   The Sacred Canopy. Garden City, N.Y.:
            Doubleday-Anchor.

    1963   Invitation to Sociology: A Humanistic
               Perspective. Garden City, New York:
               Anchor.

Berger, Peter and Luckman, T.
    1967   The Social Construction of Reality. Gar-
               den City, N.Y.: Doubleday-Anchor.

Blauner, Robert
    1964   Alienation and Freedom. Chicago: Univer-
               sity of Chicago Press.

Braude, L.
    1975   Work and Workers. New York: Praeger.

Brim, O. and Wheeler, S.
    1966   Socialization After Childhood. New York:
               Wiley.

Brooks, Nancy A. and Jeffrey W. Riemer
    1979   "Occupational Values of Artists." Heur-
               istics 9 (Spring): 69-85.

Burn, Ian
    1975   "The Art Market: Affluence and Degrada-
               tion." Artforum 12, (April): 34-37.

Burnham, S.
    1973   The Art Crowd. New York: McKay.

Chagy, Gideon
    1973   The New Patrons of the Arts. New York:
               Harry N. Abrams.

Chamberlain, Betty
    1970   The Artist's Guide to His Market. New
               York: Watson-Guptill.

Christopherson, Richard W.
    1974   "Making Art with Machines: Photography's
               Institutional Inadequacies." Urban Life
               and Culture 3: 3-34.

Design Quarterly
    1975   "The Right to a Well-Designed World."
               96: 4-12.

Durkheim, Emile
1961   "The Solidarity of Occupational Groups."
          In T. Parsons et. al. (eds.) Theories of
          Society: Foundations of Modern Sociologi-
          cal Theory, Vol. I. New York: Free Press
          of Glencoe, pp. 356-363.

Elkhoff, Marvin
1970   "The American Painter as a Blue Chip." In
          Milton C. Albrecht, James H. Barnett, and
          Mason Griff, (eds.) The Sociology of Art
          and Literature: A Reader. New York:
          Praeger, pp. 311-322.

Fox, R.C.
1957   "Training for Uncertainty." In R.K. Mer-
          ton, et. al. (eds.) The Student Physician.
          Cambridge: Harvard University Press, pp.
          207-241.

Getsels, Jacob and Csikszentmihalyi, M.
1976   The Creative Vision. New York: John Wiley
          and Sons.

Goffman, Erving
1972   "Symbols of Class Status." In Peter I.
          Rose (ed.) Seeing Ourselves: Introductory
          Readings in Sociology. New York: Alfred
          A. Knopf, pp. 203-216.

Goodman, Calvin J.
1974   "Are You a Professional Artist?" American
          Artist 38, 378: 19-21.

Gosnell, S.
1976   "Dissecting the Academic Artist." The
          Chronicle of Higher Education, May 31,
          pp. 32.

Griff, Mason
1968   "The Recruitment and Socialization of Art-
          ists." In D.L. Sills (ed.) International
          Encyclopedia of the Social Sciences, 5.
          New York: Crowell-Collier and Macmillan,
          pp. 447-454.

_____   "Conflicts of the Artist in Mass Society."
1964   Diogenes 46: 54-68.

73

1964a   "The Recruitment of the Artist." In R.N.
         Wilson (ed.) The Arts in Society. Engle-
         wood Cliffs, N.J.: Prentice Hall, pp.
         63-94.

1960   "The Commercial Artist: A Study in Con-
         sistent and Changing Identities." In M.
         Stein, et. al. (eds.) Identity and Anxi-
         ety. New York: Free Press, pp. 219-241.

1959   "Alienation and the Artist." Arts in So-
         ciety. Fall: 43-54.

Hearn, H.L.
    1972   "Aging and the Artistic Career." The Ger-
            ontologist 12: 357:362.

Hearn, H.L., Manning, P., and Habenstein, R.
    1968   "Identity and Institutional Imperatives:
            The Socialization of the Student Actress."
            Sociological Quarterly (Winter): 47-63.

Hughes, Everett C.
    1971   The Sociological Eye. Chicago: Aldine-
            Atherton.

Israel, Joachim
    1971   Alienation: From Marx to Modern Sociology.
            Boston: Allyn and Bacon.

Kavolis, V.
    1963   "A Role Theory of Artistic Interest."
            Journal of Social Psychology 60: 31-37.

Kozloff, Max
    1974   "The Authoritarian Personality in Modern
            Art." Artforum 12, 9 (May): 40-47.

Krause, Elliott A.
    1971   The Sociology of Occupations. Boston:
            Little, Brown.

Levine, E.M.
    1972   "Chicago's Art World." Urban Life and
            Culture (October): 293-322.

Mattil, Edward L.
  1971   "Art Education: A Maturing Profession."
            Art Education 24, 6 (June): 16-19.

Merrill, F.E.
  1968   "Art and the Self."   Sociology and Social
            Research: 185-194.

Meyer, Susan E.
  1974   "Can the Artist Survive in Today's Busi-
            ness World?" American Artist 38, 378
            (January): 6.

Mills, C. Wright
  1970   "Man in the Middle: The Designer."
            Architectural Design 40 (July): 363-365.

Moore, Wilbert
  1969   "Occupational Socialization." In D.A.
            Goslin (ed.) Handbook of Socialization
            Theory. Chicago: Rand McNally, pp. 861-
            883.

Myers, Bernard S.
  1957   Problems of the Younger American Artist:
            Exhibiting and Marketing in New York City.
            New York: City College Press.

Pelles, Geraldine
  1963   Art, Artists, and Society: Origins of a
            Modern Dilemma; Painting in England and
            France, 1750-1850. Englewood Cliffs,
            New Jersey: Prentice-Hall.

People Weekly
  1974   "Jamie Wyeth: A Plodding Painter." Vol.
            I, No. 13, pp. 56-61.

Poggioli, Renato
  1970   "The Artist in the Modern World." In
            Milton C. Albrecht, James H. Barnett, and
            Mason Griff (eds.) The Sociology of Art
            and Literature: A Reader. New York:
            Praeger.

Potter, Ted
  1973   "Making It in Art Outside New York." Art
            News 72 (October): 100.

Reiss, Alvin H.
  1973   "Art Education Is No Longer a Coffee Break
            for Teacher." Art News 72, 7 (September):
            30-34.

Riemer, J.W.
  1977   "Becoming a Journeyman Electrician: Some
            Implicit Indicators in the Apprenticeship
            Process." Sociology of Work and Occupa-
            tions (February): 87-98.

  1976   "'Mistakes at Work' - The Social Construc-
            tion of Error in Building Construction
            Work." Social Problems 23 (February):
            255-267.

Riesman, D.
  1968   "On Autonomy." In C. Gordon and K.J. Ger-
            gon (eds.) The Self in Social Interaction.
            New York: Wiley and Sons, pp. 445-461.

Riesman, David, Glazer, Nathan, and Denney, Revel
  1961   The Lonely Crowd. New Haven: Yale Uni-
            versity Press.

Risenhoover, M. and Blackburn, R.T.
  1976   Artists as Professors. Urbana, Ill:
            University of Illinois Press.

Ritzer, G.
  1972   Man and His Work. New York: Appleton-
            Century-Crofts.

Roe, A.
  1946   "Artists and Their Work." Journal of
            Personality 15: 1-40.

Rosenberg, Harold
  1970   "The Art Establishment." In Milton D.
            Albrecht, James H. Barnett, and Mason
            Griff (eds.) The Sociology of Art and
            Literature: A Reader. New York: Praeger,
            pp. 388-395.

Rosenberg, Bernard and Norris, E.
  1965   The Vanguard Artists: Portrait and Self-
            Portrait. Chicago: Quadrangle.

Roszak, Theodore
      1973   Where the Wasteland Ends: Politics and
                Transcendence in Postindustrial Society.
                Garden City, New York: Anchor.

Sanders, Clinton R. and Lyon, Eleanor
      1976   "The Humanistic Professional: The Reori-
                entation of Artistic Production." In Joel
                Gerstl and Glenn Jacobs (eds.) Professions
                for the People: The Politics of Skill.
                New York: Wiley, pp. 43-59.

Seeman, Melvin
      1969   "On the Meaning of Alienation." In Lewis
                A. Coser and Bernard Rosenberg (eds.)
                Sociological Theory: A Book of Readings,
                3rd edition. London: Macmillan, pp. 510-
                522.

Skiles, Jacqueline
      1975   "The National Art Workers' Community:
                Still Struggling." Art Journal 34, 4:
                320-322.

Sofer, E.G.
      1961   "Inner-direction, other-direction, and
                autonomy: a study of college students."
                Pp. 316-348 in S.M. Lipset and L. Lowen-
                thal (eds.) Culture and Social Character:
                The Work of David Riesman Reviewed.
                Glencoe, Illinois: The Free Press.

Strauss, A.
      1970   "The art school and its students: a study
                and an interpretation." Pp. 159-177 in
                M.C. Albrecht, et. al. (eds.), The Soci-
                ology of Art and Literature: New York:
                Praeger.

Upper and Lower Case: Journal of Typographics
      1976   "The Mystery of the Graphic Artist, or,
                Why 200,000,000 People Need an Art Edu-
                cation." Vol. 3, 1 (March): 1, 7-11.

Warwick, James F.
      1972   "Art Education and Public Relations."
                Art Education 25, 6 (June): 20-22.

Wayne, June
    1973   "The Male Artist as Stereotypical Female."
               Art Journal 32, 4 (Summer): 414-416.

White, Harrison C. and Cynthia A. White
    1965   Canvases and Careers: Institutional
               Change in the French Painting World. New
               York: Wiley.

Wolfe, Tom
    1975   The Painted Word. New York: Farrar,
               Straus, and Giroux.

Work in America
    1973   Cambridge, Mass.: The MIT Press.

ANNOTATED BIBLIOGRAPHY

The following represents a listing and summary of written works pertaining to art as an occupational pursuit.

Ackerman, James S.
    1969   "The Demise of the Avant-Garde: Notes on the Sociology of Recent American Art." Comparative Studies in Sociology and History, 11, 4 (October): 371-384.

This article discusses the history of innovation in art and notes that the last 20 years have seen innovation become the expected rather than the exception. The artist is no longer the outcast but an accepted member of a large class that does not allow isolation. Earlier artists gained freedom through rejection, now artists don't have that opportunity. Instead of catering to the public, the artist has moved toward the role of teacher and scientist.

Albrecht, Milton C., J.H. Barnett and M. Griff (eds.)
    1970   The Sociology of Art and Literature: A Reader. New York: Praeger.

The major sections of this reader are:
I. Forms and Styles, II. Artists (Socialization and Careers) (Social Position and Roles), III. Distribution and Reward Systems, IV. Tastemakers and Publics, V. Methodology, VI. History and Theory.

Albrecht, Milton
    1970   "Art as an Institution." In The Sociology of Art and Literature: A Reader, M. Albrecht et al. (eds.), pp. 1-23.

This article discusses various sociological approaches to art as a social institution. An interactionist, conflict, and functionalist approach are used to illuminate the social relationships of artist-critic-audience; the consequences of art work for society; and the location of art within the larger social structure.

Anton, John P.
   1968   "The Role and Dilemma of the Contemporary
           Artist." Buffalo Studies, IV, 4 (December):
           71-106.

This article compares existential theories about
the nature of art and its relationship to humanness.
The artist's dilemma lies between being a whole
person while among corrupting institutions. Survival could lead to corruption by the institutions
of society. To meet this dilemma the artist has
created a new self image based upon concentrated
subjectivism - inward action (self presentation)
coupled with outward action (defense against non-
artistic demands).

Becker, Howard S.
   1974   "Art as Collective Action." American So-
           ciological Review 39: 767-776.

This article suggests that people cooperate to
produce a work of art. The network of people involved in the making of art lends itself to the
study of collective social action. Social organization consists of the special case in which the
same people act together to produce a variety of
different events in a recurring way.

Bell, Quentin
   1970   "Conformity and Nonconformity in the Fine
           Arts." In Sociology of Art and Literature:
           A Reader, M. Albrecht, et al. (eds.), pp.
           687-701.

This article suggests that the nonconforming painter of today is still conforming. When the rule becomes change and ingenuity, nonconformity becomes
conformity. If an artist provides a public what
it wants - change and innovation, then the artist's
role is based upon conformity. The author feels
that the artist of the future will be indistinguish-
able from other persons in society and the creative
genius of the artist may disappear.

Bensman, Joseph and Israel Gerver
1970   "Art and the Mass Society." In Sociology
of Art and Literature: A Reader, M. Albrecht, et al. (eds.), pp. 660-668.

This article traces the historical relationship
between the artist and his market. Once the artist and patron were familiars and shared tastes,
but the rise of the middle class created a mass
market. Now the artist is distant from the con-
sumer. Public taste defines art work, restricts
innovation, and determines development.

Burn, Ian
1975   "The Art Market: Affluence and Degrada-
tion." Artforum 13, (April) 34-37.

This article discusses the economic pressures
placed on artists by the art market. Art work is
viewed as a commodity that is bought and sold.
The price of an art product has little to do with
production costs. Rather, the artist is just another producer in the labor force who is involved
in a purely impersonal, economic relationship.
Artists are forced to create marketable products
with little regard to personal depth or expression. This situation has alienated the artist
from his work.

Burnham, Sophy
1973   The Art Crowd. New York: McKay.

This book deals with art politics through an in-
side description of money and power in the art
world of New York. Some of the myths surrounding
artists are discussed as are the social relationships between artists, art dealers, art critics,
museum curators, and collectors. The business of
art is multifaceted and problematic for the artist.

Chamberlain, Betty
1970   The Artist's Guide to his Market. New
York: Watson-Guptill.

A sourcebook for artists. The chapters include:
1) Are you ready to exhibit?, 2) Galleries and
how they function, 3) Shopping for a Gallery, 4)

Showing work to dealers, 5) Business terms and agreements, 6) Pricing and selling, 7) Publicity, 8) Cooperative galleries, 9) Artist groups and organizations, 10) Exhibiting without gallery or group affiliation, 11) Miscellaneous tips and observations.

Christopherson, Richard W.
1974   "Making Art with Machines: Photography's Institutional Inadequacies," Urban Life and Culture 3: 3-35.

This article discusses the role and status of the fine art photographer. Photography lacks the institutional structures within the art world that would provide artistic justification and economic viability. Currently, photography is not recognized as an art form. The problems facing the fine art photographer are discussed.

Elkhoff, Marvin
1970   "The American Painter as a Blue Chip." In The Sociology of Art and Literature: A Reader, M. Albrecht et al. (eds.) pp. 311-322.

Artists have often lived under the myth of extreme poverty. Now, many artists are making money. They have been thrown into a celebrity life style and are no longer protected from the corruption of success. Many artists of today have compromised their creativity of art for recognition and success. This compromise has led many artists to become more attentive to their audiences - catering to them with quickly changing art styles.

Getzels, Jacob W. and Mihaly Csikszentmihalyi
1976   The Creative Vision: A Longitudinal Study in Art. New York: John Wiley.

This book reports on a study of artists in art school and again several years after graduation. The authors distinguish between "problem-finding artists" and "problem-solving" artists" and track the successfulness and career lines of these groups. Emphasis is placed on both the cognitive processes in art and the socio-cultural pressures on artists.

Goodman, Calvin J.
    1974   "Are You a Professional Artist?" American
            Artist 38, 378: 19-21.

The article questions whether artists are professional and suggests that they are not because
they do not provide specialized services for a
salary or fee. Artists are seen as necessary for
society but unsupported. Artists are compared to
independent businessmen who operate primarily
"on speculation" without a knowledge of business
skills.

Gosnell, S.
    1976   "Dissecting the Academic Artist." The
            Chronicle of Higher Education May 31,
            p. 32.

The academic artist is viewed as a special person
who does not have an objective subject. The
quality of art work is based upon opinion not objective evaluation. No one can tell a person how
to do art since art is so subjective. Academic
artists have only their imagination to offer.

Griff, Mason
    1959   "Alienation and the Artist." Arts in So-
            ciety Fall: 43-54.

Alienation occurs when the members of a group no
longer share the same values as the rest of their
society. Since the discontinuation of the patronage system artists have felt increasingly alienated from society. This article traces the socio-
historical context of the artists' plight.

Griff, Mason
    1960   "The Commercial Artist: A Study in Chan-
            ing and Consistent Identities." In M.
            Stein, et al. (eds.) Identity and Anxiety,
            New York: Free Press, pp. 219-241.

The dilemma of the design artist is discussed as
a role strain between the values of art and the
values of making a living. An identity shift is
required for artists deciding to pursue a career
in commercial art. The discussion centers on the
role conflict faced by commercial artists and the
mechanisms used to reduce this conflict.

Griff, Mason
    1964   "Conflicts of the Artist in Mass Society."
            Diogenes 46: 54-68.

    This article discusses the complexities between
    advertising art and pure art. The training of
    the artist involves the selection and socializa-
    tion into an appropriate role. Three roles - 1)
    fine artist, 2) commercial artist, and 3) a com-
    promise role are suggested and the problems asso-
    ciated with each are illuminated.

Griff, Mason
    1964a   "The Recruitment of the Artist." In The
            Arts in Society, R.N. Wilson (ed.), Engle-
            wood Cliffs, N.J.: Prentice-Hall, pp. 63-
            91.

    Based upon interviews with art students in Chi-
    cago this article explores the reasons why an art
    career is chosen. Art schools induce students
    with scholarship programs. Persons may be en-
    couraged by their peer group or influential oth-
    ers. Both positive and negative inducements are
    discussed.

Hearn, H.L.
    1972   "Aging and the Artistic Career." The Ger-
            ontologist 12: 357-362.

    This article focuses on the aging artist and
    those who take up art in their later years. Many
    artists see the later years as a beginning of
    creativity or an expanding of it because of an in-
    crease in leisure time. Art work can become an
    income for the retired person as well as a satis-
    fying pursuit.

Krause, Elliott.
    1971   The Sociology of Occupations. Boston:
            Little, Brown. Chapter 10, Science and
            the Arts.

    This chapter views science and the arts as cre-
    ative occupations, then describes their differ-
    ences and similarities. Focus is on creativity
    which permeates both fields. Artists are more

likely to confront society's whole meaning system
through their work.

Levine, E.M.
　　1972　"Chicago's Art World." Urban Life and
　　　　Culture (October): 293-322.

This article discusses the Chicago art world and
its reliance upon the New York art world. Chicago's art distribution system is dependent upon
1) the nature of the product, 2) the New York influence, and 3) the leading gallery dealers, museums and collectors. The Chicago system is limited to initiating artist's careers. New York
offers success.

Mattil, Edward L.
　　1971　"Art Education: A Maturing Profession."
　　　　Art Education 24, 6 (June): 16-19.

This article suggests that in recent years art
education has drifted away from the production of
art to art appreciation. Discussion focuses on
the recent federal funding of the arts and how the
direction of art education has changed as a result
of this.

Meyer, Susan E.
　　1974　"Can the Artist Survive in Today's Busi-
　　　　ness World?" American Artist 38, 378 (Jan-
　　　　uary): 6.

This article suggests that the world sees the artist as a bohemian who disdains money and who is
not really working. Since society does not take
artists seriously they become alienated. The author suggests that artists should learn business
practices that will place them on an equal level
with business minded laymen and thereby achieve
the prosperity they deserve.

Mills, C. Wright
　　1970　"Man in the Middle: The Designer." Arch-
　　　　itectural Design 40 (July): 363-365.

This article discusses the design artist as a businessperson caught between two great developments in American society: the shift in economic emphasis from production to distribution coupled with a drive for status and the subordination of art, science and learning institutions to the dominating economic institutions. As a result, the design artist is confronted with insecurity, frustration and guilt. Mills suggests that craftsmanship should be held as the highest human ideal.

Potter, Ted
　　1973　　"Making It in Art Outside New York." Art
　　　　　　News 72 (October): 100.

This article discusses the major problems facing the Midwest artist. Suggestions are offered.

Rosenberg, Bernard and Norris Fliegel
　　1965　　The Vanguard Artist: Portrait and Self-
　　　　　　Portrait. Chicago: Quadrangle Books.

Based on interviews with 29 successful New York painters and sculptors the authors attempt to describe the social and psychological factors that influence artists' work. A cultural view of the New York art world is also provided as the context in which their work takes place. Problems facing the modern artist are discussed.

Sanders, Clinton R. and Eleanor Lyon
　　1976　　"The Humanistic Professional: The Reorien-
　　　　　　tation of Artistic Production." In Joel
　　　　　　Gerstl and Glenn Jacobs (eds.) Profes-
　　　　　　sions for the People: The Politics of
　　　　　　Skill. New York: Wiley, pp. 43-59.

This article defines the professional artist as a person who defines himself (herself) as a professional, creates works of art for money as an occupation, and is aware of a colleague group which evaluates his work. The "traditional artistic professional" and the "new artistic professional" are compared. The "traditional artistic professional" is apart from mainstream society, disdains commercial artists, and depends upon the economic

elite for livelihood while conflicting with their
values. They encourage the mystique bestowed upon
them by the public. The "new artistic professional," on the other hand, seeks to demystify himself
by becoming economically independent from the economic elite, emphasizes the art process rather
than the art product and encourages alternative
artistic institutions.

Strauss, Anselm
    1970   "The Art School and Its Students: A Study
            and an Interpretation." In M.C. Albrecht,
            et al. (eds.) The Sociology of Art and
            Literature. New York: Praeger, pp. 159-
            177.

This article is based on interviews with 70 art
students and recent graduates. The results are
based on a single art school. The art school is
seen as a sorting device for placing recruits into
artistic occupations in society. Various student
"types" are delineated and compared.

Wayne, June
    1973   "The Male Artist as a Stereotypical Fe-
            male." Art Journal 32, 4 (Summer):
            414-416.

This article suggests that male artists are viewed
within a woman's role by the larger society. Several similarities are discussed: male artists are
viewed as relatively powerless, overly emotional,
having mysterious powers of insight, and strong
dependence on others for economic survival.

White, Harrison C. and Cynthia A. White
    1965   Canvases and Careers: Institutional Change
            in the French Painting World. New York:
            Wiley.

This book provides an interesting combination of
art history and sociology to explain the emergence
of French painting. The art institutions existing
today have their roots grounded in the social process and social structures portrayed here.

ABOUT THE AUTHORS

JEFFREY W. RIEMER is an Associate Professor of Sociology at Wichita State University. He received Bachelor's and Master's Degrees from the University of Wisconsin - Milwaukee and a Ph.D. from the University of New Hampshire, all in sociology. He is the author of Hard Hats - The Work World of Construction Workers (SAGE, 1979) and numerous articles in sociological journals. His research and teaching interests focus on work and the moral order.

NANCY A. BROOKS, Assistant Professor of Sociology, teaches at Wichita State University where she also received her B.A. and M.A. degrees in sociology. She is the author of several professional research articles in the areas of disability and chronic disease. Art and the world of artists have been lifelong interests.